TOMBSTONE
THE FIRST FIFTY YEARS
1879 TO 1929

BY
DON TAYLOR

FOR MY MOM, DAD AND FAMILY

WITH SPECIAL GRATITUDE AND THANKS TO THE MANY WONDERFUL PEOPLE WHO HAVE INSPIRED AND SUPPORTED ME IN MY RESEARCH...

BUT THE JOURNEY ISN'T OVER YET.

© 2010 Old West Research & Publishing, L.L.C.
All Rights Reserved

CHAPTER ONE

Many pages and miles of film have been dedicated to writing about a place that has become synonymous with the American Old West, Tombstone, Arizona. Beginning in the 1920's, historians, tourists and writers began to journey there to touch history. This town had had it all. Silver mining brought the masses in the early 1880's seeking instant wealth with one swing of the pick or scoop of a shovel. Like most mining camps, the merchants, restaurateurs and other "service providers" quickly followed. However, this mining camp would see an additional element of men migrate to the area, the men who called themselves "Cowboys." These men were not drawn to the region by the allure of precious metals. Their migration into the Arizona Territory was one of ironic survival.

In the spring of 1878, Ed Schieffelin and his two partners, Albert Schieffelin and Richard Gird arrived in Southeastern Arizona Territory, and began to work the silver claims Ed had discovered the year before. That same year, the "Cowboys" relocation to this same area was forced by the then President of the United States, Rutherford B. Hayes. President Hayes had issued the Presidential Proclamation that precedes declaring Martial law in the Territory of New Mexico. Governmental corruption and the Lincoln County War had attracted hordes of outlaws into New Mexico. President Hayes had no other recourse except to threaten the Territory with the authorized use of Federal troops to enforce the law. As communities began to develop around the Tombstone mines and stamp mills, the "Cowboys" settled on ranches surrounding these canvas villages, and provided beef at less than market rates with cattle stolen from Mexico. It was a perverse supply and demand scenario. The "Cowboys" supplied the beef the growing population demanded through rustling. But as these settlements grew into cities and towns, and the rich silver ore was transformed into bullion, the "Cowboys" began to demand the supply.

Tombstone received its territorial charter as a city in 1881. In three short years the population had grown to over 3500, the minimum requirement for this designation. That same year a new county was formed, Cochise County, and Tombstone was chosen as the County Seat. 5925 square miles of Pima County were carved out along the borders of New Mexico Territory and Mexico. The staple of the economy was precious metals, primarily silver. Tombstone had become a thriving metropolis. That year telephones were installed between the Grand Central and Contention mines, and they would be installed within the city the following year. Plans for the County Courthouse, City hall and an opera house were being implemented. Two newspapers reported the events of the day. The hotels, restaurants and saloons were decorated with the most lavish and modern fixtures available. Churches and schools began to organize and the citizens constructed equally modern structures for these institutions. Soon the most sought after entertainers and theatrical troupes would perform in a variety of halls and venues. In what had been the unexplored heart of the Chiricahua Apaches' land, a prolific city was emerging.

Yet in the areas surrounding Tombstone, the pioneer farmers and ranchers faced a daily menace that had not affected the cities and towns. They called themselves "Cowboys." The outlaws had a network of branches throughout the southeastern region of the Arizona Territory and ready reinforcements from nearby New Mexico Territory and Texas. They committed heinous crimes against the citizens and governments of both the United States and Mexico; then they used the international border as a shield from the respective law enforcement agencies. The matter was very simple for the government of Mexico. They demanded that the United States government arrest the outlaws immediately and bring these perpetrators to justice. The Arizona Territorial Government in Prescott also looked to Washington, D.C., for assistance in resolving this dilemma. However, the solution would not be forthcoming from Capitol Hill. In fact, both President Chester A. Arthur and his Cabinet failed to comprehend that the "Cowboys" were no merely a band of cattle thieves; they were an early form of an organized crime syndicate. In almost every community, the "Cowboys" outnumbered the local authorities, as well as any potential posse these authorities could assemble. Their reputations as gunmen, as well as their expertise in the tactic of ambushing their adversaries, made them a far superior force; one that could not be underestimated. The only resource that could equal or better the outlaws was the U.S. Army. However, the Posse Comitatus Law of 1878, which applied to not only states but Federal territories, prevented all military personnel from taking any enforcement action against United States citizens unless under a Presidential Order of Martial Law. This two year old piece of legislation from the previous administration and the U.S. Attorney General's misconstruction of the formidable force his subordinates were facing caused confusion, misinterpretation and, most of all, delay in providing Mexico and the Territory of Arizona with a solution to their problem.

The U.S. Attorney for Arizona Territory during this time was E. B. Pomroy. In a letter to the U.S. Attorney General, Wayne McVeigh, Pomroy defined the outlaws and described the current state of affairs with neighboring Mexico as follows:

Letter from E. B. Pomroy to Wayne McVeigh, June 23, 1881

Courtesy of The National Archives and Records Administration Publication Number: M2028 Publication Title: Records Relating to U.S. Marshal Crawley P. Dake, the Earp Brothers, and Lawlessness and 'Cowboy Depredations' in Arizona Territory, 1881-85. Record Group Number: 60 Record Group Title: General Records of the Department of Justice
National Archives II, College Park, Maryland

Pomroy went on to request that the Attorney General provide sufficient funding for the U.S. Marshal for the Arizona Territory, Crawley Dake, to recruit and field a posse to arrest these "freebooters." Pomroy's mention of the "exiled ranger from Texas" can only be one man, John Slaughter. Slaughter had migrated from Texas, where he had been a member of the Texas Rangers, to Lincoln County, New Mexico with a herd of cattle. The hands he brought with him, and that followed him westward, were equally quick with a lariat as well as a gun. In 1879, the New Mexico Territorial Governor, Lew Wallace, compiled a list of the "Most Wanted Men" in his territory for the U.S. Secretary of the Interior, and John Slaughter was #1. It should be noted that William Bonney, Tom O'Folliard, and Charlie Bowdre were numbers 14 through 16 respectively. Seeking greener grass and a cleaner slate, John Slaughter and his men moved to the San Bernardino Land Grant, which originated in far southeastern Arizona Territory and extended into Mexico. Slaughter's part in the events that would unfold involving the Earp brothers and the "Cowboys" is conspicuously and inexplicably missing from the historic records. He is seldom in Tombstone during the Earp brother's turbulent 28-month residency, yet he is mentioned frequently as a visitor in Charleston, which was located further west of Tombstone. This little burg sprang up across the San Pedro River from Millville, Richard Gird's original center for milling and processing silver ore. Gird did not allow alcohol in his town, so Amos Stowe founded Charleston which would become the western center of operations for the "Cowboys" and Galeyville, located on the eastern slopes of the Chiricahua Mountains was their headquarters on the eastern side of Cochise County. Between these two towns, the "Cowboys" set up their scheme of ranches throughout the valley. The hubs of this network would be the original Clanton Ranch, four miles south of Charleston, the second McLaury Ranch, located near Soldier's Hole Springs, and the second Clanton Ranch, purchased and occupied by Newman Haynes "Old Man" Clanton near Las Animas, New Mexico Territory.

Approximate Ranch Locations
Author's Collection

CHAPTER TWO

In the fall of 1879, Wyatt Earp had joined his brother Virgil in Prescott, Arizona Territory. News of the booming new silver town had also drawn the oldest brother, James, to this locale. With plans for opening a stagecoach line in Tombstone, the brothers and their families began their journey south. On December 1, 1879 they arrived in the new mining Mecca. The Earps' dreams of becoming transportation magnates quickly dissipated when they discovered two existing stagecoach lines in Tombstone in the midst of a price war. Perhaps as a contingency plan, Virgil had been appointed U. S. Deputy Marshal by Crawley Dake, the U.S. Marshal for Arizona Territory, prior to leaving Prescott. There is a distinct possibility that Wyatt was also deputized at this time, but Crawley Dake kept no records during his tenure as U.S. Marshal for Arizona. The provenance for this statement will unfold as the story unfolds. Crawley Dake was a man of many parts as they used to say. Newspapers provide most of the records of his deputy appointments. Joseph W. (J.W.) Evans, the Deputy U.S. Marshal in Tucson, seemed to act as Dake's liaison with the Mexican Consul in Tucson, as well as the Governor of Sonora, Luis Torres. Evans had only one arm, so it is not clear if his role was purely political or if he actually participated in fieldwork. In Tombstone there were at least two U.S. Deputy Marshals, Leslie F. Blackburn and Virgil W. Earp. Blackburn's primary duties were as a Customs Collector for Wells Spicer, the U.S. Court Commissioner for the first district of the Arizona Territory (Southeastern Arizona). This left Virgil Earp with the responsibility of enforcing all other Federal laws in this region. It is interesting to note that we have record of numerous communiqués between Dake, Evans and the U.S. Attorney General, but there are almost no documents to and/or from Virgil Earp, who was closest to the epicenter of the Cowboy criminal activity. Although Dake would later be investigated for embezzlement, his intentions in the case of pursuing and arresting the "Cowboys" appear to be legitimate. He understood the urgency and magnitude of this task, but he was never able to effectively convey these issues to his superiors. As early as August of 1880, the citizens and investors in Tombstone realized the threat the "Cowboys" posed to the future of their city and Cochise County. This small item appeared in the Epitaph:

IN VIEW OF THE LARGE ELEMENT OF BAD, AND IN MANY INSTANCES, DANGEROUS CHARACTERS, IN OUR MIDST, WE LEARN THAT THE BUSINESS MEN AND PROPERTY OWNERS ARE SERIOUSLY CONSIDERING THE EMPLOYMENT OF A SECRET SERVICE OFFICER TO KEEP WATCH OF THEM. WE THINK THE IDEA AN EXCELLENT ONE, AND WE HAVE A PARTY IN OUR MIND'S EYE WHO IS PARTICULARLY WELL QUALIFIED BY PREVIOUS TRAINING TO FILL THE PLACE.

Tombstone Epitaph, April 14, 1880

As with many blurbs and items in the newspapers of Tombstone, there is no further mention of this clandestine idea. The identity of the "party" is not clear.

Virgil would fall back on the low-paying U.S. Deputy Marshal's job, while James quickly returned to his vocation of bartender and saloon operator. Wyatt would return to the familiar position of shotgun messenger for Wells Fargo & Co., but on July 27, 1880, he would be appointed by Pima County Sheriff Charles Shibell to serve as his deputy in Tombstone. Morgan, who had arrived that spring, assumed the duties of Wells Fargo messenger. Tombstone's first true tragedy struck on October 28, 1880 when City marshal Fred White responded to the sound of gunshots below the lot at 6th and Allen Street. Here White found "Curly" Bill Brocius and demanded his pistol. As White pulled the weapon from Brocius' hand it fired sending the bullet into White's lower abdomen. Wyatt did not usually carry a firearm, and that evening he was playing cards in this manner. Upon hearing the shots he borrowed a pistol and rushed to the scene in time to see Marshal While fall mortally wounded. Wyatt hit Brocius over the head and secured both the pistol and the prisoner. Brocius was quickly transported to the County Seat in Tucson for fear that a vigilance committee may form and lynch the perpetrator. White held on for two more days and in his dying declaration, White said the shooting was accidental. This was attested by Wyatt and gunsmith Jacob Gruber at Brocius' hearing in Tucson, and charges were dismissed.

Wyatt would serve commendably as Pima County Deputy Sheriff according to both newspapers. However, this service would only last until the next election in November of that year. Shibell was a Democrat, but he did not let political affiliations influence his hiring choices. He sought the best man for the position. Wyatt, on the other hand, was a Republican. Because he chose to support Shibell's Republican challenger, Bob Paul, in the race for Sheriff, Wyatt decided to resign his post rather than appear hypocritical by campaigning for his employer's opponent. Two days after his resignation was accepted, on November 11, 1880 John Behan was appointed as Wyatt's replacement. With the accolades for Wyatt appearing in both newspapers on the same day Shibell announced Behan's selection as the new Deputy, perhaps this initiated the rivalry that would develop in the coming months between the two men. After all, the standard of performance had been publicized and all eyes would be on Behan to see if he would fill Wyatt's shoes. During all of the local political turmoil, the movement to create a new county with the booming Tombstone as its seat of government was on the fast track in the Territorial Legislature. On February 1, 1881 the new Cochise County was formed. Tombstone, as expected, was designated as the County Seat, and John Behan was appointed as its first Sheriff.

As the silver bullion gushed toward the capitalist centers like San Francisco, the "Cowboys" became more brazen and brutal in their cattle venture. On March 15th of 1881, the "Cowboys" attempted to expand their enterprise into the arena of highway robbery. Four men tried to stop the stagecoach between Contention City and Benson, its final destination. Eli "Budd" Philpot manned the reins with Bob Paul riding beside him as the Wells Fargo & Co. shotgun messenger. Four masked men called out, "Hold!" Paul replied, "By God, I hold for nobody," and let go a volley from his shotgun. More shots rang out and Philpot was mortally wounded, as was passenger Peter Roerig, who was riding in the jump seat. Philpot was well loved by the residents of both Tombstone and his home in Napa Valley, California. He was considered by his employer, Wells Fargo & Co., to be a stellar driver. Almost immediately a posse was formed to hunt down the four cold-blooded outlaws that had killed this dedicated family man. The posse was a formidable one, consisting of Morgan, Virgil and Wyatt Earp, Bat Masterson, Bob Paul, John Behan, and Marshall Williams, the Tombstone Wells Fargo Agent. The posse followed the outlaws' tracks to a ranch owned by Leonard Redfield. Here they found a shady character named Lew King, who proved to be one of the four fugitives. In spite of Wyatt's edict to sequester King from Redfield, Behan stood by as the two chatted. After interrogating King, Behan was tasked with taking the desperado to jail in Tombstone. The events that followed would reveal Behan's true allegiance. King was escorted to the County Jail in Tombstone and placed in the custody of the new Under Sheriff, Harry Woods. On March 28, 1881, Woods was instructed to place the prisoner in chains. Fifteen minutes later, Lew King walked out the back door of the County Jail to a waiting horse and he escaped. Behan's failure to isolate King at the Redfield Ranch, and the careless handling of the prisoner served notice that he and his office found it safer to collect licenses and taxes than to enforce the law.

**John H. Behan
Author's Collection**

The subsequent action by Wells Fargo & Co. and the Territory of Arizona would have significant repercussions six months later. These two entities issued a reward for the capture of Harry Head, Bill Leonard and Jim Crane in the amount of $1,200.00 per man. Today Wells Fargo claims they never offered more than $300.00 for any criminal until Butch Cassidy, but as they say, a picture is worth a thousand words.

Don't post, but place in the hands of discreet and reliable persons only.

$3,600 00 REWARD.

ARREST THE MURDERERS!

About 9 o'clock Tuesday evening, March 15, 1881. the stage bound from Tombstone to Benson was attacked by three men armed with Winchester rifles, at a point about two miles west from Drew's stage station, and Budd Philpot, the driver, and Peter Roerig, a passenger, shot and killed.

The attack was no doubt made for the purpose of robbery. The Territory and Wells, Fargo & Co. have a liberal standing reward for the arrest and conviction of persons robbing or attempting to rob the Express. In addition, the Governor and Wells, Fargo & Co. have each offered $300 for the arrest and conviction of each of the murderers of Philpot and Roerig, so that the rewards now offered amount to $1,200 or $1,400 each.

It is believed that the attempted robbery and murders were committed by Bill Leonard, Jim Crain and Harry Head, described as follows:

BILL LEONARD.

American; about 30 years old; about 5 feet, 8 or 9 inches high; weight, 120 lbs.; long, dark, curly hair, when cared for hanging in ringlets down to shoulders; small, dark, boyish mustache, otherwise almost beardless; teeth very white and regular; dark eyes; small, sharp and very effeminate features; rather weak voice; left arm full of scars caused by injecting morphine; is subject to rheumatism; chews tobacco incessantly; speaks good Spanish; good shot with rifle and pistol; a jeweler by trade; is known in Silver City, Otero and Los Vegas, N. M.

JAMES CRAIN.

American; about 27 years old; about 5 feet, 11 inches high; weight, 175 or 180 lbs.; light complexion; light, sandy hair; light eyes; has worn light mustache; full, round face, and florid, healthy appearance; talks and laughs at same time; talks slow and hesitating; illiterate; cattle driver or cow-boy.

HARRY HEAD.

About 18 or 20 years old; 5 feet, 4 or 5 inches high, weight, 120 lbs.; chunky and well built; dark complexion; dark hair and eyes; rather dandyish; almost beardless; small foot and hand; good rider, and handy with rifle and pistol.

All mounted, and well armed with rifles and pistols, and the last trace of them they were going toward San Simon Valley.

If arrested, immediately inform Sheriff Behan and the undersigned by telegraph at Tombstone, A. T.

R. H. PAUL,
Special Officer of W., F. & Co.

Tombstone, A. T., March 23, 1881.

Author's Collection

CHAPTER THREE

The summer of 1881 would be the pinnacle of lawlessness in Cochise County. The first major incident occurred when a butcher named McAllister from Galeyville, a small mining town on the eastern slopes of the Chiricahua Mountains would secure the contract to supply beef to Fort Bowie. He and his cronies named George Turner, Garcia and Oliver went to Mexico with approximately $3,000.00 to purchase the cattle. All of these men had ties with the "Cowboys". The Tombstone Daily Nugget newspaper carried this piece on June 9, 1881:

Tombstone Daily Nugget, June 9, 1881

Twenty days later this tidbit was printed in the "Local Intelligence" column, about area happenings and points of interest, of the same paper:

> **Those Cow-Boys.**
> On Sunday evening last Hon. P. R. Tully received word from Col. Biddle, commanding Camp Grant, that he had received information that "Bi-lp the Kid" and 25 cow-boys had been seen in the vicinity of the Big Cienega, going toward Fronteras. The news was at once imparted to general Morales, and a courier dispatched to Fronteras with the intelligence. The Consul infored a Journal reporter that he felt no apprehension as to any damage the cow-boys may do except to scatter ranches. Even these are very well guarded by about 250 troups of the Mexican regular army.—Journal.

Tombstone Daily Nugget, June 29, 1881

Crawley Dake was the U.S. Marshal for the Arizona Territory during these turbulent years. Based on the available correspondence, it appears that Joseph W. Evans, the U.S. Deputy Marshal in Tucson was not only Dake's "lead" deputy, but he also served as liaison to the Mexican Ambassador and government. Evans proved to be a very reliable and steadfast deputy despite having only one arm. Although the timing of the previous newspaper reports may be suspect in relation to the actual events, the following letter from Evans describes the current state of affairs between the United States of America and Mexico:

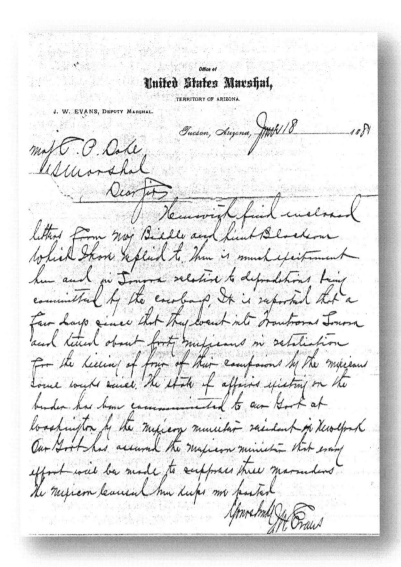

Letter from J. W. Evans to Crawley Dake, June 18, 1881
Courtesy of The National Archives and Records Administration Publication Number: M2028 Publication Title: Records Relating to U.S. Marshal Crawley P. Dake, the Earp Brothers, and Lawlessness and 'Cowboy Depredations' in Arizona Territory, 1881-85. Record Group Number: 60 Record Group Title: General Records of the Department of Justice
National Archives II, College Park, Maryland

Evans outlines how the party of "Cowboys", seemingly described in the June 29th Daily Nugget, invaded Fronteras,

Sonora, Mexico. A few days prior to the date of this letter, the outlaws took revenge for the killing of McAllister and the other three men, by murdering forty Mexican citizens on the streets of their hometown. When the U.S. and local authorities failed to send out a posse of any kind after the perpetrators, the "Cowboys", like most criminal outfits, knew that Cochise County and the Mexican State of Sonora were their domain. With no fear of retribution, the "Cowboys" were fearless of law enforcement from either side of the international border.

**Crawley Dake, U.S. Marshal, Arizona Territory
Author's Collection**

Next is a letter from the Governor of Sonora, Luis Torres, which documents another attack by the "Cowboys" on Mexican Nationals:

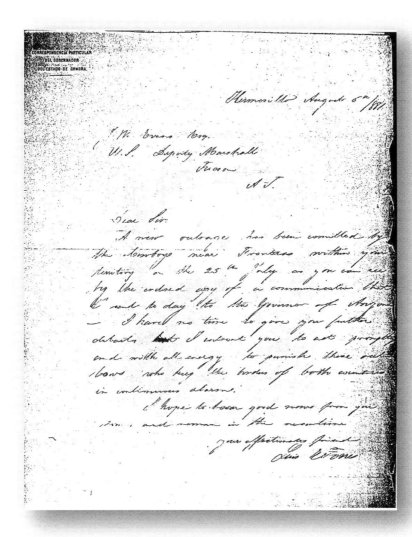

Letter from Luis Torres to J.W. Evans, August 6, 1881

Courtesy of The National Archives and Records Administration Publication Number: M2028 Publication Title: Records Relating to U.S. Marshal Crawley P. Dake, the Earp Brothers, and Lawlessness and 'Cowboy Depredations' in Arizona Territory, 1881-85. Record Group Number: 60 Record Group Title: General Records of the Department of Justice
National Archives II, College Park, Maryland

The only newspaper item reporting a clash between the "Cowboys" and Mexican nationals is dated August 3, 1881 and has quite a different spin on the incident.

Cattle Thieves Routed

From Bob Clark, who recently returned from New Mexico, the NUGGET learns that about the 26th of last month, a party of Mexicans from Sonora, made a raid into the Animas and adjoining valleys, and rounding up several hundred animals, started with them through the Guadaloupe Pass for Mexico. The Mexicans numbered about thirty all told. The cattlemen organized about twenty in number, and pursuing the marauders, overtook them on the plains near the Pass. A running fight ensued, which resulted in the flight of the Mexicans, and the recovery of the cattle. He also states that in Skull Canyon he struck a pack train of about thirty mules which had evidently been stampeded, as their packs were turned upside down, and there was no one in charge of them. He expresses the opinion that the train was a smuggling one from Sonora, and that the owners had been attacked by the Rustlers, and killed, and the train had stampeded during the melee. It is reported that a smuggling trail leads through this neighborhood, and that very often trains are taken in by the marauders who infest that country. The Mexicans can make no complaint to the authorities, being engaged in an unlawful business themselves.

Tombstone Daily Nugget, August 3, 1881

On August 1, 1881 the bandits would strike again. The Daily Nugget carried this story:

An Interrupted Breakfast:
Report comes to us of a fresh outrage perpetrated by the cow-boys in Sonora. Early last Monday morning a party of sixteen Mexicans from the interior of Sonora on their way to this Territory to purchase goods and carrying $4000 for that purpose, stopped at a curve in the road at Los Animas, near Fronteras, to prepare their frugal breakfast. While busily engaged preparing their tortillas they were saluted with music of twenty rifles fired by cow-boys who lay in ambush awaiting them. The Mexicans took this as an invitation to leave and did not stand on the order of their going but left all their mules and pack saddles in which they carried their money for the purchase of goods. When they stopped running they were at Fronteras and their party was four short. The missing men are supposed to have been killed. The citizens of Bablspe and troops are after the cowboys and are disposed to take summary vengeance if they overtake them. —Tucson Citizen.

A gentleman arrived in Tombstone yesterday, it is said, who verifies the above story, however, we have not seen him and can not vouch for the truth of the report.

Tombstone Daily Nugget, August 5, 1881

J.W. Evans notified U.S. Marshal Crawley Dake of the tragedy.

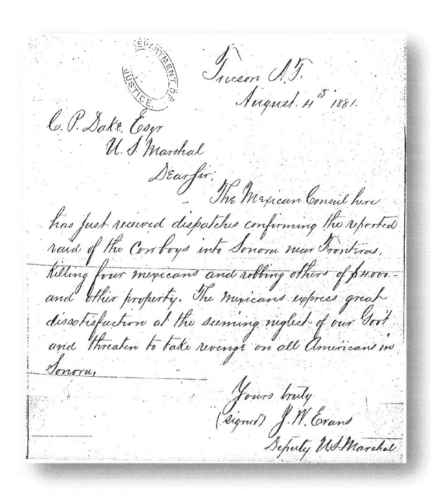

Letter from J. W. Evans to Crawley Dake, August 4, 1881

Courtesy of The National Archives and Records Administration Publication Number: M2028 Publication Title: Records Relating to U.S. Marshal Crawley P. Dake, the Earp Brothers, and Lawlessness and 'Cowboy Depredations' in Arizona Territory, 1881-85. Record Group Number: 60 Record Group Title: General Records of the Department of Justice
National Archives II, College Park, Maryland

The next communiqué was sent to the U.S. Attorney General by Dake the next day, and it is with this message that the mystery of the Earps' role in Tombstone begins.

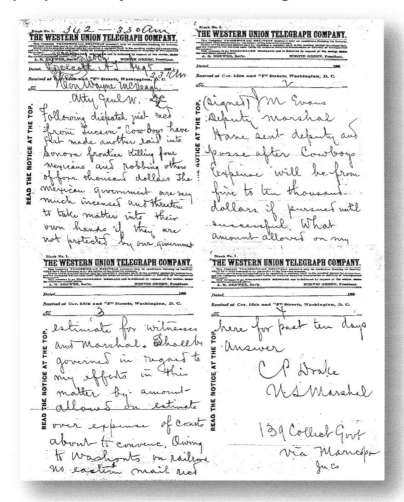

Telegram to Wayne McVeigh, U.S. Attorney General from Crawley Dake, August 5, 1881

Courtesy of The National Archives and Records Administration Publication Number: M2028 Publication Title: Records Relating to U.S. Marshal Crawley P. Dake, the Earp Brothers, and Lawlessness and 'Cowboy Depredations' in Arizona Territory, 1881-85. Record Group Number: 60 Record Group Title: General Records of the Department of Justice
National Archives II, College Park, Maryland

On page 2, Crawley Dake states that he had sent a Deputy and a posse out after the perpetrators, but he fails to identify the men. The location of the attack was in Skeleton Canyon, which runs from Mexico, through the Arizona Territory and into the New Mexico Territory. Again, based on the correspondence, the "Cowboys" committed another heinous crime in the State of Sonora, Mexico. The modern value of the loot would be over $180,000.00, not an insignificant sum.

This offense sparked a new flurry of communication between the Mexican government, the Territorial government and the Federal government, as well as between the members of Chester Arthur's Cabinet. J.W. Evans' letter of August 10th carries two important pieces of information, an educated estimate of the number of outlaws, and the fact that Mexican troops have mobilized.

Tucson Arizona Aug 10" 1881

Maj. C. P. Dake
U.S. Marshal

Dear Sir,

Yours of 5" inst at hand. Herewith find enclosed letter from Gov Torres and official communication from him to Gov of Arizona. The Mexican authorities are becoming very much incensed at our seeming neglect in suppressing the depredations of the Cowboys. I am doing everything in my power to assure them of our good intentions in this matter. I wrote to Gov Torres to day explaining to him the unavoidable delay that has occurred and assuring him of speedy action on our part. The Consul here exhibits much feeling over the outrages inflicted upon his people and country by the Cowboys but says he has hopes we will do something soon. I have explained the matter fully to him. Gov Torres informs me that there are three hundred soldiers on the border of Sonora who will render us every assistance possible. The Mexican Consul does not think it possible for them to obtain the names of the cowboys

Letter from J.W. Evans to Crawley Dake, August 10, 1881

Courtesy of The National Archives and Records Administration Publication Number: M2028 Publication Title: Records Relating to U.S. Marshal Crawley P. Dake, the Earp Brothers, and Lawlessness and 'Cowboy Depredations' in Arizona Territory, 1881-85. Record Group Number: 60 Record Group Title: General Records of the Department of Justice
National Archives II, College Park, Maryland

Governor Torres notifies Evans that 300 soldiers have been sent to protect the border against what Evans estimates is 75-100 "Cowboys". He does add the caveat that there are ready reinforcements available to the gang from New Mexico and Texas. This sets the stage for an incident that remains controversial to this day.

On August 13, 1881 as the sun peaked over the canyon rim, a barrage of gunfire hammered the campsite of Newman H. (Old Man) Clanton, Jim Crane (the last man wanted for killing Budd Philpott), William Lang, Charlie Snow, Harry Earnshaw, William Byers, and Richard Gray. In a matter of moments, five of the seven men lay dead, and the two wounded outlaws did not move for fear of being discovered still living. Clearly, the August 16th report of the incident shows there was no remorse for Jim Crane's death.

MORE BORDER TROUBLES.

Mexicans on a Raid—Five men Killed Including the Notorious Jim Crane.

About half-past four o'clock last evening news reached town that Dick Gray, youngest son of M. Gray, of our city, and well known here, had been killed together with four others, by Mexicans near the town of Gillespie, New Mexico. The news caused considerable excitement and knots of curious inquirers gathered about the streets, eager to hear the particulars. About an hour later Andy Ames and Joe Trebble arrived in town from the scene of the murders and confirmed the news. There are several reports as to the causes that led to this lamatable affair. The immediate particulars are about as follows: A party consisting of Wm. Lang, Dick Gray, Jim Crane, Charles Snow, the senior Clanton, Wm. Beyers and Harry Ernshaw, camped last Friday night in the Guadalupe canyon about 110 miles east from Tombstone and very near to the Mexican line. Early on Saturday morning the party were attacked by Mexicans and Lang, Gray, Crane, Snow and Clanton were killed. Beyers escaped with a wound in the abdomen, while Ernshaw ran away amidst a shower of bullets one of which grazed his nose. It is estimated that the Mexican party numbered from 27 to 30 men. The condition of the camp indicated that the attack was made just as the murdered men were about getting up; one had evidently been killed while yet laying down.

Jim Crane, it will be remembered, was concerned in the murder of "Budd" Philpot. He joined the fated party, we are informed, at midnight, Friday and was only camped with them for the night. He was a fugitive from justice and an outlaw and the six bullets that struck him were certainly well expended. Wm. Lang was a young man about 22 years of age and had been in that section of the country with his cattle about three months. In conversation with his father last evening our reporter learned that the two came to Arizona from Kansas about five months ago. They are men of large capital, have had an extended experience in the stock business and intended putting about 10,000 head of cattle on their range, had it not been for these border troubles. The son was bringing in some beef cattle for the Tombstone market when killed. Mr. Lang leaves today to see that his son's body is properly buried and to remove all cattle to some less troubled spot.

It is certainly lamentable that the men should be slain with the stock, yet this was nothing more than was to be expected as a result of the raids from both sides of the line. For example: we understand that a party of "rustlers," as they are called, went down into Mexico last month and rounded up some cattle. They were followed by the Mexicans who got so close upon them that they were obliged to abandon the stock. This was done in the vicinity of the late murder. The Mexicans took the stock and started back for home, at the same time picking up such cattle and horses as they chanced to meet. The stock was missed and a party of 16 Americans started in pursuit, overtook the Mexicans, had a fight with them and retook the stock. This occurred during the latter part of July. If this is true it is probable that the recent raiders were some of the same party defeated last month. Be this as it may, we know there are bad characters on both sides who will continue to engender strife and bloodshed, and that immediate and positive measures should be adopted to eliminate this evil and protect the peaceful and industrious citizens.

Tombstone Daily Epitaph, August 16, 1881

The unsettled question is who killed the bandits? Historic records indicate that it was the Mexican Rurales, a loosely organized militia used to patrol the international border. However, if this had been the case, the ambush would have been an armed invasion of a territory of the United States by the military of a foreign power. In his 1995 book "Tombstone, A.T." William Shillingberg states that there are no records in Sonora indicating any kind of authorized military action on either side of the border on this date. Yet the survivors stated later they saw Mexican troops mutilating and stripping the bodies of their dead comrades. All of this contradiction brings us back to Crawley Dake's telegram dated August 5, 1881, in which he declared he had sent a deputy and posse out after the "Cowboys". The closest U.S. Deputy Marshal was Virgil Earp, and it is likely that his posse consisted of his brothers Wyatt, Morgan, Warren, "Doc" Holliday, and any other close allies Virgil could rely on. The Mexican troops may have been simply observers to the first action the United States Government took against the outlaws. If the Rurales had engaged the seven men on American soil, there would have been a huge outcry from the citizens of Cochise County, but more from the military commanders in the area. Yet as you will see from the following telegram copies, the Army dispatched troops to the Mexican border as a policing action to prevent Americans from crossing over into Mexico seeking retribution.

Copy.
5037 A.G.O. 1881.

Telegram.
Pacific Division
August 22, 1881.

Repeats dispatch from Comdg Genl. Dept of Arizona giving information that the Mayor of Tombstone reports the killing of a party of Americans (said to be Cowboys) by Mexicans in Guadaloupe Canyon and that large parties are starting for Mexico to retaliate. Has not been called upon by civil authorities who are unable to prevent retaliation; but has ordered troops to the border to prevent violation of neutrality laws. and stating that military are powerless to act under the Posse Commitatus law.

Official Copy

A.G. Office }
Aug 24/81 }

Adjutant General

For the Honorable
The Attorney General.

War Dept.

Department of Justice.

Received: Aug 26, 1881

Dated: " 26, 1881

From: Robt T Lincoln
      Secy

SUBJECT:

Copy of telegram from Comdg Genl Div. of the Pacific in relation to the killing of a party of Americans in Guadalupe Canon &c

ACTION:

War Department
Washington City
August 25th, 1881.

I have the honor to enclose herewith copy of telegram dated the 22nd instant from the Commanding General Division of the Pacific, repeating one from the Commanding General of the Department of Arizona, informing him that the Mayor of Tombstone reports the killing of a party of Americans in Guadaloupe Cañon, and that large parties are starting from Mexico to retaliate; also that he has ordered troops to the border to prevent any violation of the neutrality laws.

A similar copy is furnished this day to the Honorable Secretary of State.

    Very respectfully,
    Your obedient servant,
    R*b*m*o* Lincoln
    Secretary of War.

The Honorable
The Attorney General.

Presidio of San Francisco Cal.
August 22nd 1881.

Adjutant General
Washington D.C.

Following telegram received from Commanding General Department of Arizona: —

"Clum the Mayor of Tombstone reported seventeenth Killing of party of Americans by Mexicans in Guadaloupe Canyon and starting of large parties from Tombstone and vicinity for Mexico in retaliation."

These reports are confirmed from Camp Huachuca and Fort Bowie, the Mayor of Tombstone asks what steps the Military have taken. I have not been called upon by civil authorities for assistance to make arrests as in the case contemplated by Attorney General, but have ordered troops to be sent to the border to intercept all armed parties raiding into Mexico with hostile intent and disarm them, or if found returning, to aid the civil authorities to arrest them. The troops seem powerless to act under the posse comitatus law, and local Commanders have done nothing beyond seeking information and reporting. The last parties killed are said to be Cowboys, but the sympathy of the border people seem to be with them and I doubt whether any local civil authorities can, or will do anything to prevent retaliation.

(Sgd) Kelton.
A.A.G.

**Telegram from Robert Lincoln to U.S. Attorney General,
August 26, 1881**

Courtesy of The National Archives and Records Administration
Publication Number: M2028 Publication Title: Records Relating to
U.S. Marshal Crawley P. Dake, the Earp Brothers, and Lawlessness
and 'Cowboy Depredations' in Arizona Territory, 1881-85. Record
Group Number: 60 Record Group Title: General Records of the
Department of Justice
National Archives II, College Park, Maryland

Instead the following is a telegram reporting the next attack.

Telegram from A.A.G. Kelton to Adjutant General

Courtesy of The National Archives and Records Administration
Publication Number: M2028 Publication Title: Records Relating to U.S. Marshal Crawley P. Dake, the Earp Brothers, and Lawlessness and 'Cowboy Depredations' in Arizona Territory, 1881-85. Record Group Number: 60 Record Group Title: General Records of the Department of Justice
National Archives II, College Park, Maryland

CHAPTER FOUR

Cochise County in the Arizona Territory was quickly turning into an international powder keg with a lit fuse. Yet, the City of Tombstone was flourishing and growing daily. Here are some articles describing the lavish hotels and saloons businessmen had built in Tombstone as described in the Tombstone Epitaph.

THE GRAND HOTEL

THROUGH THE COURTESY OF MR. H. V. STRUM AN EPITAPH REPORTER YESTERDAY PAID A VISIT TO AND MADE A BRIEF INSPECTION OF THE NEW CHIRSTENED THE GRAND WHICH WILL BE FORMALLY OPENED FOR DINNER THIS EVENING AT FIVE O'CLOCK. THE GENERAL SIZE AND CHARACTER OF THE STRUCTURE HAVE BEEN MENTIONED SO OFTEN DURING THE COURSE OF CONSTRUCTION THAT FURTHER MENTION WOULD BE SUPERFLOUS AND WE WILL CONFINE OURSELVES TO A DESCRIPTION OF THE INTERIOR APPOINTMENTS OF IT. PASSING INTO THE BUILDING BY THE FRONT ENTRANCE THE FIRST THING THAT STRIKES THE EYE IS A WIDE AND HANDSOME STAIRCASE COVERED BY AN ELEGANT CARPET AND SUPPORTING A HEAVY BLACK WALNUT BALISTER. THENCE UPSTAIRS TO THE MAIN HALL, AND TURNING TO THE RIGHT WE ARE USHERED INTO A PERFECT LITTLE BIJOU OF COSTLY FURNITURE AND ELEGANT CARPETING KNOWN AS THE BRIDAL CHAMBER. THIS ROOM OCCUPIES HALF OF THE MAIN FRONT AND IS CONNECTED WITH THE PARLOR BY FOLDING DOORS THROUGH WHICH THE REPORTER PASSED, AND ENTERING THE PARLOR WAS MORE THAN ASTONISHED BY THE LUXURIOUS' APARTMENTS. A HEAVY BRUSSELS CARPET OF THE MOST ELEGANT STYLE AND FINISH GRACES THE FLOOR; THE WALLS ARE ADORNED WITH RARE AND COSTLY OIL PAINTINGS; THE FURNITURE IS OF

WALNUT CUSHIONED WITH THE MOST EXPENSIVE SILK AND REP, AND NOTHING LACKS, SAVE THE PIANO WHICH WILL BE PLACED IN POSITION SHORTLY. ON DOWN THROUGH THE MAIN CORRIDOR PEEPING NOW AND THEN INTO THE BEDROOMS, SIXTEEN IN NUMBER, EACH OF THEM FITTED WITH WALNUT FURNITURE AND CARPETED TO MATCH; SPRING MATTRESSES THAT WOULD TEMPT EVEN A SYBARITE, TOILET STANDS AND FIXTURES OF THE MOST APPROVED PATTERN, THE WALLS PAPERED, AND TO CROWN ALL, EACH ROOM HAVING WINDOWS. ALL ARE OUTSIDE ROMS THUS OBVIATING THE MANY DISCOMFORTS IN CLOSE AND ILL-VENTILATED APARTMENTS. RETURNING WE PASS DOWN THE BROAD STAIRCASE AND TURNING TO THE LEFT ARE IN THE OFFICE AND READING ROOM. HERE WE MET MR. R. J. PRYKE, THE POLITE AND AFFABLE CLERK, SO WELL KNOWN TO YOSEMITE TOURISTS IN CALIFORNIA. THE OFFICE FIXTURES ARE AS IN COMMON IN FIRST CLASS HOTELS AND FULLY IN KEEPING WITH THE GENERAL CHARACTER OF THE HOUSE. THE DINING ROOM ADJOINING NEXT INVITES INSPECTION. HERE WE FIND THE SAME EVIDENCE OF GOOD TASTE IN SELECTION AND ARRANGEMENT THAT IS SO MARKED A FEATURE OF THE WHOLE INTERIOR. THREE ELEGANT CHANDELIERS ARE PENDANT FROM THE HANDSOME CENTERPIECES; WALNUT TABLES, EXTENSION AND PLAIN, COVERED WITH CUT GLASS, CHINA, SILVER CASTORS AND THE LATEST STYLE OF CUTLERY ARE AMONG THE MANY ATTRACTIONS OF THIS BRANCH OF THE CUSINE.

  THENCE INTO THE KITCHEN WHERE WE FIND THE SAME EVIDENCE BEFORE MENTIONED; AN ELEGANT MONTAGIN RANGE 12 FEET IN LENGTH, WITH PATENT HEATERS, HOT AND COLD FAUCETS, IN FACT ALL THE APPLIANCES NECESSARY TO FEED FIVE HUNDRED PERSONS AT A FEW HOURS NOTICE ARE PRESENT. THE BAR OCCUPIES THE EAST HALF OF THE MAIN FRONT AND IS IN KEEPING WITH THE GENERAL FURNISHINGS. WANT OF SPACE PREVENTS

MORE THAN THIS CURSORY GLANCE AT THE GRAND AND ITS APPLIANCES FOR THE COMFORT AND CONVENIENCE OF GUESTS. A GRAND (NO PUN INTENDED) INVITATION BALL WILL TAKE PLACE THIS EVENING.

Tombstone Epitaph September 9, 1880

THE TOMBSTONE CLUB

THE ELEGENT BOOKS OF THE TOMBSTOEN CLUB, IN THE SECOND STORY OF THE RITCHIE BUILDING WERE THROWN OPEN TO THE MEMBERS LAST EVENING. A CASUAL GLANCE AT THE ROUGH UNPLASTERED WALLS AND CRUDE STAIRWAY ON THE EXTERIOR, WOULD NOT LEAD ONE TO BELIEVE THAT SUCH TASTE AND ELEGANCE REIGNED WITHIN. THE MAIN SITTING ROOM OF THE CLUB IS 19 X 45 FEET, TASTEFULLY FURNISHED WITH WRITING AND CARD TABLES, EASY CHAIRS AND READING TABLES. THE FLOOR IS CARPETED WITH RICH BRUSSELS CARPET, LARGE PATTERN AND YELLOW THE PREDOMINATING COLOR. THE UNITY OF COLOR IN THE FURNISHING OF THE ROOM IMMEDIATELY ATTRACTS ATTENTION. THE CHAIRS, CUSPADORES AND CURTAINS ARE OF THE SAME GENERAL COLOR AS THE CARPET, WHICH HAD THE EFECT OF MAKING THE APPEARANCE MORE PLEASING TO THE EYE THAN HETROGENEOUS BLEND OF HUES. A MAGNIFICENT SIDEBOARD, WELL LADENED WITH CHOICE LIQUORS AND CIGARS IS NOT THE LEAST ATTRACTIVE PORTION OF THE FURNITURE. A SPACIOUS APARTMENT IN THE REAR OF THE READING ROOM WILL BE SUBDIVIDED IN CARD, STORE AND WASH ROOMS IN A FEW DAYS. THE CLUB HAS ABOUT SIXTY MEMBERS, AND IS IN A VERY FLOURISHING CONDITION. MORE THAN SEVENTY PUBLICATIONS, COMPRISING ALL OF THE LEADING AMERICAN AND FOREIGN, NEWSPAPERS, MAGAZINES AND PERIODICALS ARE RECEIVED. TO MR. RICHARD

RULE, WHO HAS HAD CHARGE OF FURNISHING THE ROOMS AND ARRANGING THEM, THE CLUB IS INDEBTED FOR A DISPLAY OF ELEGANT TASTE AND GOOD JUDGMENT.—

Tombstone Epitaph September 29, 1880

THE ALHAMBRA SALOON

TOM CORRIGAN, THE GENTELMANLY AND COURTEOUS PROPREITOR OF THIS WELL KNOWN TOMBSTONE SALOON SHOULD HAVE BEEN MORE THAN PLEASED AT THE CROWD THAT GREETED HIS REOPENING ON SATURDAY EVENING LAST. HIS FRIENDS, AND THEY ARE LEGION, CROWDED THE SPACIOUS APARTMENTS FROM EARLY EVE UNTIL FAR INTO THE MORNING, AND OVER BREAKERS OF FOAMING HEIDSICK WELCOMED HIS RE-ENTRE. TO THE OLD HABITUES OF THE ALHAMBRA THE CHANGE IS A MARKED ONE. THE FIRST THING GREETING THE EYE IS THE NEW BAR, OF BLACK WALNUT HANDSOMELY MOUNTED WITH BIRDS-EYE MAPLE. THE GLITTERING ARRAY OF DECANTERS AND GLASSES ORNAMENTING THE SAME, PRESENTS A SCENE OF ARTISTIC BEAUTY THAT MUST BE SEEN TO BE APPRECIATED. ON THE WALLS OF THE BAR AND READING ROOM ARE TASTEFULLY ARRANGED MANY ELEGANT PAINTINGS AND ENGRAVINGS, COPIES OF THE GREAT MASTERS. THE CHANDELIERS ARE OF BRONZE AND GOLD, AND WHEN LIT AST SUCH A FLOOD OF DAZZLING LIGHT OVER THE SURROUNDINGS AS TO LEAD T0O THE IMPRESSION THAT ALLADIN'S CAVE HAD BEEN REDISCOVERED AND WE ARE IN THE MIDST OF IT. THE CEILING HAS BEEN RAISED ALSO AND THE WALLS COVERED WITH PAPER OF ELEGANT DESIGN. AN ORCHESTRA OF THREE PIECES DISCUSSES THE LATEST AND MOST FASHIONABLE MUSIC. THE GAMBLING TABLES, THREE IN NUMBER, ARE SURROUNDED BY CROWDS

OF EAGER TO TEMPT THE FICKLE GODDESS. BEHIND THE BAR, PLEASANT AND SMILING STAND ANDY ROBERTSON AND L.A. HEARY SUPPLYING WITH THEIR WELL KNOWN SKILL THE THIRSY THRONG, WHILE EVER AND ANON TOM'S GOOD NATURED FACE CAN BE SEEN AS HE GREETS WITH FRIENDLY HAND SHAKE SOME OLD TIME FRIEND. THE STOCK OF LIQUORS AND CIGARS CANNOT BE EXCELLED IN ARIZONA. EVERYTHING IN THIS LINE HAS BEEN PROCURED REGARDLESS OF EXPENSE AND WITH THE EYE SINGLE TO TASTE OF HIS NUMEROUS PATRONS. THE OPENING WAS IN EVERY SENSE A GRAND SUCCESS AND ARGUES WELL FOR THE ALHAMBRA AGAIN RESUMING THE PLACE IT OCCUPIED PRIOR TO TOM'S VISIT EAST.—

Tombstone Epitaph September 14, 1880

THE ORIENTAL SALOON

FOR SEVERAL WEEKS PAST THE SPACIOUS CORNER BUILDING OF THE VIZINA & COOK BLOCK HAS BEEN UNDERGOING NUMEROUS FINISHING TOUCHES PREPARATORY OF ITS OCCUPATION BY MESSRS. M.E. JOYCE & CO., THE GENERAL PROPRIETORS OF THE SOON-TO-BE-FAMOUS ORIENTAL. LAST EVENING THE PORTALS WERE THROWN OPEN AND THE PUBLIC PREMITTED TO GAZE UPON THE MOST ELEGANTLY FURNISHED SALOON THIS SIDE OF THE FAVORED CITY OF THE GOLDEN GATE. TWENTY EIGHT BURNERS SUSPENDED IN NEAT CHANDERLIERS AFFORDED AN ILLUMINATION OF AMPLE BRILLIANCY, AND THE BRIGHT RAYS REFLECTED FROM THE MANY COLORED CRYSTALS ON THE BAR SPARKLED LIKE A DECEMBER ICELING IN THE SUNSHINE. THE SALOON IS COMPRISED OF TWO APARTMENTS. TO THE RIGHT OF THE ENTRANCE IS THE BAR, BEAUTIFULLY CARVED, FINISHED IN WHITE AND GILT AND CAPPED WITH A HANDSOMELY

POLISHED TOP. IN THE REAR OF THIS STAND A BRACE OF SIDEBAORDS WHICH ARE SIMPLY ELEGANT AND MUST BE SEEN TO BE APPRECIATED. THEY WERE MADE FOR THE BALDWIN HOTEL, OF SAN FRANCISCO, BUT BEING TOO SMALL, MR. JOYCE PURCHASED THEM. THE BACK APARTMENT IS COVERED IN BRILLIANT BRUSSELS CARPET, AND SUITABLY FURNISHED AFTER THE STYLE OF A GRAND CLUB ROOM, WITH THE CONVENIENCE OF WILY DEALERS IN POLISHED IVORY. THE SELECTION OF FURNITURE AND FIXTURES DISPLAYS EXQUISITE TASTE, AND NOTHING SEEMS TO HAVE BEEN FORGOTTEN___EVEN A HANDSOME STOCK OF STATIONARY. TOMBSTONE TAKES THE LEAD AND MESSRS. JOYCE & CO. OUR CONGRATULATIONS.

Tombstone Epitaph, July 22, 1880

A catastrophic fire in many of 1881 would destroy many of these wondrous structures, but the business district, the town would rebuild and even expand. Plans were in the works for the new Cochise County Courthouse to house the county government. A permanent City Hall was being designed. Al Schieffelin and W.A. Harwood had begun construction of an opera house that would rival any venue west of the Mississippi River. It was almost as if Tombstone was in a dome of prosperity, while the rest of the county was under siege by the "Cowboys".

The "Cowboys" revenge for the killing of Old Man Clanton and others would continue into August of 1881. The following appeared in the August 20, 1881 Daily Nugget.

> Frank Leslie returned Thursday night from a sojourn of a couple of months in southwestern New Mexico. On his return to Tombstone he came by way of Guadaloupe Cañon, and was among the first on the ground of last week's massacre. At Blackwater, this side of there, he found the bodies of three dead Mexicans, but recently killed, which would indicate that the work of retribution has already commenced.

Tombstone Daily Nugget, August 20, 1881

That very same day, the Nugget carried an editorial which indicates that war with Mexico was not an issue being discussed in Washington, D.C. exclusively. It is not clear whether the author of this piece was trying to simply put a positive spin on a grave situation, or if they were naïve to the effects of war, or if their arrogance was so great that they truly felt Tombstone and the country could and would benefit from this international conflict.

THE DAILY NUGGET.

TOMBSTONE, AUGUST 20, 1881.

WHAT WILL BE ITS EFFECTS?

Many and various are the conjectures indulged in as to what will be the effect upon Southern Arizona in case of a war with Mexico. While there is a general disposition of sympathy with the Mexicans in their losses and sufferings occasioned by the marauding exploits of the thieves that infest portions of the Territory, there is an equally general feeling of indignation that American soil should be invaded by a squad of Mexican soldiery—it now appears certain that the recent massacre in Guadaloupe Canyon was perpetrated by such—and innocent parties slaughtered in retaliation. While many, for various reasons, would wish to see a war avoided, the more candid admit that it appears almost inevitable, and hence are discussing the questions created by the query above, both as regards American interests at home and in Mexico.

It is not doubted that the effect will be disastrous upon the latter interests for the time being, but as our interests there are mainly mining, all present evil effects will be remedied by the greater facility afforded in the future for development of mines and their manipulation in other respects—proceeding always upon the only reasonable hypothesis that Mexico will be conquered and her northern States annexed to our Union. Space does not permit of any extended review of the obstacles now existing to all American enterprises in Mexico, but they are grave and numerous. That the hopes of those who have labored long and faithfully there must be longer deferred is a matter of regret, but the fruition will be but the more full when the hour for it arrives.

As to the direct effects here, they are more difficult to be foreseen. Many mining enterprises will be checked and the inauguration of others postponed, the timidity of capital preventing its entrance where war is holding carnival. But the mines already being worked profitably will scarcely be shut down. There is not great danger that any towns upon the American side will be attacked, and if the tide of battle should drift near us, proximity to the railroad will give security. Commercial enterprises will be greatly quickened, for in addition to the military forces that will draw somewhat upon our local establishments for supplies, immigration to the country will be largely increased. True, this augmentation of our population will not be of a class in the main greatly desired, but still they will have a tendency to increase business. These minor effects will probably be all that can be noted. The prices of our mining stocks will not be affected, nor our bullion output greatly lessened. What delay may be occasioned by the temporary stoppage of the influx of capital, will be compensated for by the increased activity in other branches. So that a reasonable and legitimate reply to the prevailing question is that the existing condition of things will not be materially altered during the continuance of the trouble. At its close, with the inevitable attendant victory of the Americans, the throwing open of an extensive country, and one reported to be highly favored by nature, will tend to the benefit of the established American towns along the border.

Tombstone Daily Nugget August 20, 1881

As the "dog-days" of summer were lingering in 1881, the lines of the condemnation and support for the "Cowboys" were becoming clearer. The point of differentiation was seemingly defined by political affiliation. The majority of the outlaws were Southern Democrats, while most of the Earps and the corporate/mining investment community were Northern Republicans. Even the newspapers reflected political opposition with the Nugget touting the Democratic platform and the Epitaph supporting the Republican Party line. These lines were also drawn between those who profited from the "Cowboys" criminal activity and those who did not. Yet in spite of his complete lack of performance during the summer-long crime spree, Behan remained securely in office.

Behan's appointment to replace Wyatt as Pima County Deputy Sheriff had been somewhat of a surprise being a Democrat selected by a Republican Territorial Administration. His move to Cochise County Sheriff was not a political promotion. Wyatt Earp also wanted to be the county's first Sheriff. Behan was not confident that he could overcome a direct competition with Wyatt, so he approached him with a proposition. If Wyatt would withdraw from consideration for the office of Sheriff, Behan, if selected, would name Wyatt as his Under-Sheriff and the two would split the tax collection commissions equally. Since Behan had performed his duties well as Pima County Deputy Sheriff and had not revealed his susceptibility toward corruption, Wyatt accepted his proposal. It wasn't until Wyatt returned from the initial chase for Leonard Head and Crane in March of 1881, that he learned that Behan had double-crossed him and named Harry Woods as his Under-Sheriff. This was the origin of the personal dispute between the two men. It was also a foreshadowing of the path Behan would follow in the coming months.

As the fall months of 1881 approached, Tombstone was rapidly reaching a state of normalcy. Businesses had been rebuilt or were very near completion. Mining production was still progressing at a skyrocket pace.

Telephones had been installed between the Grand Central and the Contention mines, and plans were being made to install a telephone exchange throughout the city. The population and the profits continued to grow exponentially in spite of the increased threat of war due to the outlaws in Cochise County. In Washington, D.C., the administration was rebuilding from President Garfield's assassination under the guidance of Chester A. Arthur. President Arthur's role in the Cochise County state of affairs would become another mystery in the history of Tombstone. There are several stories that will be outlined late that appear to directly involve the President of the United States in these episodes. However, these stories will remain just stories because they can never be proven or disproven. Any provenance could only be found in President Arthur's documents and papers. Chester Arthur burned his papers the day before he died.

President Chester A. Arthur
Author's Collection

CHAPTER FIVE

Although the calendar had reached the autumn months of 1881, Cochise County, A.T. was still hot and Washington, D.C. was a hotbed of correspondence. Despite the summer's rampant attacks by the "Cowboys", the Federal Government was reeling in a paradox from the previous administration called The Posse Comitatus Act. During the final years of Reconstruction following the Civil War, this issue remained a stumbling block for politicians. The Republicans relented on the matter in order to elect Rutherford B. Hayes. As President, Rutherford B. Hayes signed The Posse Comitatus Act, which prevents any military force from taking any action against a citizen of the United States, unless under an order of martial law by the President. Thus the only group in Arizona Territory that could match the "Cowboys" man-for-man was the only entity that could do nothing to stop them. The outlaws were very aware of this and their rampage continued.

After months of bloodshed, the first active step toward stopping the "Cowboys" was taken. On September 5, 1881, J.W. Evans sent a letter to Crawley Dake itemizing the cost of putting a posse of "qualified" deputies in pursuit of the "Cowboys". The fact that no official had drafted this form of proposal prior to this date is another one of the many mysteries surrounding the United States Government's passive behavior. Granted the President's Cabinet and the country had been in turmoil since the death of President Garfield, but no one but the military demonstrated any sense of urgency in seeking a solution to the "Cowboy" dilemma. It should be noted that Evans includes military personnel in his posse estimate. This was a shrewd tactic, because if the "Cowboys" chose to engage the posse, the military could have taken an active role if fired upon first. U.S. Marshal Dake forwarded this letter to Washington, D.C. where the new Acting Attorney General, S. F. Phillips, responded with an equally mystifying message:

Tucson Sept 5"

Maj C. C. Dodd
U.S. Marshal
Dist of Ariz

Yours of 1" inst at hand, I reply as to what my idea is concerning the probable cost of a contemplated expedition against the cowboys I herewith submit the following. I think it advisable to take sufficient force to prevent the possibility of defeat in case of engagement (the latter I consider inevitable) A force of two hundred (200) including soldiers Indians and citizens will I think be sufficient. The citizen force should not be less than thirty (30) men who are worth hiring cannot be had for less than $10.00 per day and expenses everything furnished them. Good horses cannot be had for less than $100.00 each, besides these a number of pack animals will be necessary. Saddles bridles saddles blankets will cost about twenty five dollars ($25.00) for each horse. I do not know what the arms will cost they cannot be had here. Each man should have a carbine & two pistols. I think it advisable to be prepared to remain in the field at least thirty days, we may be much longer. A greater number of citizens than thirty (30) are desirable

Letter from J.W. Evans to Crawley Dake, September 5, 1881

Courtesy of The National Archives and Records Administration Publication Number: M2028 Publication Title: Records Relating to U.S. Marshal Crawley P. Dake, the Earp Brothers, and Lawlessness and 'Cowboy Depredations' in Arizona Territory, 1881-85. Record Group Number: 60 Record Group Title: General Records of the Department of Justice
National Archives II, College Park, Maryland

This response is dated October 17th:

> I AM IN RECEIPT, BY YOUR RESPONSE, OF A COMMUINICATION FROM J.W. EVANS O YOU DATED TUCSON SEPTEMBER 5, 1881 IN RELATION TO THE PROBABLE COST OF A CONTEMPLATED EXPEDITION AGAINST THE COW-BOYS. I OBSERVE THAT MR. EVANS ESTIMATES THAT THE COST OF SUCH AN EXPEDITION WILL AMOUNT TO ABOUT THIRTY THOUSAND DOLLARS. IF THAT BE SO THERE IS NO SUFFICIENT APPROPRIATION AT MY DISPOSAL APPLICABLE TO THE PURPOSE OF BREAKING UP THE ORGANIZATION AND SUITABLE ACTION BY CONGRESS MUST BE AWAITED.

Letter from S. F. Phillips, Acting Attorney General to Crawley Dake, October 17, 1881

Courtesy of The National Archives and Records Administration Publication Number: M2028 Publication Title: Records Relating to U.S. Marshal Crawley P. Dake, the Earp Brothers, and Lawlessness and 'Cowboy Depredations' in Arizona Territory, 1881-85. Record Group Number: 60 Record Group Title: General Records of the Department of Justice
National Archives II, College Park, Maryland

By now the situation was complete chaos, and bordering comical. The primary men in the field had finally requested sufficient funding to rid the area of the outlaws, only to discover that the amount needed more than the Presidential Cabinet member in charge of the Department of Justice could afford. The frustration Dake and Evans must have felt, had to be overwhelming. Fortunately, this information never reached the citizens of Arizona Territory or the Mexican Government. This one scenario is indicative of the bureaucratic bedlam going on in Washington.

The Acting Governor, John Gosper, had reported that there were 380-400 "Cowboys" ransacking Cochise County. In reality there were probably 75-100, but still Dake and his deputies were powerless. On September 10, 1881 the daily Nugget would carry two important articles side-by-side.

Tombstone Daily Nugget, September 10, 1881

The first outlines the failed attempt by U.S. Deputy and City Marshal Virgil Earp to shoot a fleeing Sherman McMasters, who was wanted by Sheriff Bob Paul in Pima County. The irony is that Virgil missed McMasters with five, maybe six shots after finishing second in a marksmanship contest the week before. The second article details the robbery of the stagecoach, from Tombstone to Bisbee, the latest addition to the "Cowboys" enterprise. By expanding their criminal activity to include stagecoach robbery, the "Cowboys" also broadened the scope of jurisdiction for these crimes. The stagecoaches carried the U.S. Mail, and by rifling through and stealing the mail, they were now breaking Federal Laws. They also incurred the wrath of Wells Fargo & Company, who dispatched their best Detectives, John Thacker and James Hume. These two men were responsible for the capture of the notorious "Black Bart" in the California gold country. Hume's arrival, though, was less than auspicious. The stagecoach he was on in route to Tombstone was robbed and the thieves took his pair of brand new Smith & Wesson Schofield pistols. The "Cowboys" would strike once too often between Tombstone and Bisbee. The result, Wells Fargo & Co. would close the route after losing $6000.00 in payrolls in less than thirty days.

The circumstances were building in and around Tombstone. Federal authorities could not make a decision on how to deal with the outlaws in southeastern Arizona Territory. The County Sheriff, John Behan, had demonstrated his unwillingness to perform his duty. U. S. Marshal Crawley Dake could not get the funds necessary to bring the criminals to justice, and now their offenses were falling under his jurisdiction. The events from March 18, 1881 when the "Cowboys" killed Budd Philpott to the present were leading the key local players toward an inevitable collision course.

CHAPTER SIX

When John Behan lost Lew King, his first major prisoner as Cochise County Sheriff, Wyatt looked to capitalize on the situation and on the greed of the "Cowboys." He approached several of them including Joe Hill, Frank McLaury and Ike Clanton to lure Bill Leonard, Harry Head, and Jim Crane back to Cochise County where Wyatt could arrest them, and gain a tremendous advantage over Behan in the next election for Sheriff. In return, the outlaws would receive the $3600.00 reward ($1,200.00 for each man) being offered for the three. Today that would be equal to about $54,000.00, and apparently it was enough or Joe Hill and Ike Clanton, for they agreed to the plan. Ike's paranoia would broaden the circle of those who knew the plan. He wanted Wyatt to confirm that the reward would be paid on these outlaws dead or alive. Wyatt wired Wells Fargo & Co. and the answer came back, "Yes, dead or alive." The telegram had to be sent through Marshall Williams, the Tombstone Wells Fargo & Co agent. Williams saw Wyatt take the information to Ike, and he realized something was going on. Before Hill could reach Leonard and Head, the Haslett brothers killed them in New Mexico for the reward, and the "Cowboys" summarily killed the Haslets before they could collect a penny. When Jim Crane was killed with Old Man Clanton in Guadalupe Canyon, the whole plan fell apart. Hill was not a significant player, but Ike Clanton was. If his comrades in crime found out he had intended to inform on the three, he would soon join them all.

On October 24, 1881, Ike and Tom McLaury rode into to Tombstone. Ike had been worried for months after Marshall Williams made a drunken comment about the scheme. Ike was concerned that "Doc" Holliday had been told by Wyatt. "Doc" had been in Tucson when Morgan arrived to bring him back to Tombstone on October 20th. Upon his arrival, Wyatt asked "Doc" if he had heard anything, and of course, "Doc" replied negatively. At this point Wyatt told him about the plan, and on the evening of

October 25th "Doc" and Ike met at the Alhambra saloon. Holliday immediately called Ike a "damned liar." The argument continued for several minutes until Morgan was asked to step in as a Special Deputy City Marshal. Virgil reached the scene as Morgan escorted both men out of the Alhambra, split the two up and sent them on their way. Now Ike's terror was being fueled by anger and alcohol. Later he pulled Wyatt from his faro game at the Eagle Brewery, and said he was not armed when "Doc" berated him, but that he would be in the morning. Wyatt ignored Ike's drunken threat and told him to go sleep it off. Eventually Ike found his way to a poker game with Virgil, Tom McLaury and John Behan which lasted the remainder of the night. At the conclusion of the game, Ike again threatened "Doc" and wanted Virgil to deliver the challenge. Virgil had the same response as his brother, and ignored Ike's inebriated babble. While the Earp brothers slept, Ike continued his "tour" of the saloons and his drinking binge.

Virgil and Wyatt awoke late in the morning on October 26th to the warnings of friends that Ike was armed and roaming the streets looking for each or all of the brothers and Holliday. Tombstone is located on a small mesa 4530 feet above sea level. That morning it was cloudy, cold blowing rain and snow. Wyatt wore his overcoat with a specially lined pocket for his revolver. The Earps went out that morning to stop Ike from causing any _real_ trouble. In 1880, before Virgil was appointed to replace the deceased Fred White as Town Marshal, the City Council had passed this ordinance making it illegal to carry weapons within the city limits without a permit.

> **DAILY EPITAPH.**
> PIONEER DAILY OF THE CAMP.
> SATURDAY MORNING, AUGUST 14, 1880
>
> **CITY ITEMS.**
>
> **Carrying Concealed Weapons.**
> As there seems to be great divergency of opinion regarding the wording of the municipal ordinance in relation to the carrying of concealed weapons, we publish it entire.
>
> ORDINANCE NO. 9.
>
> Be it ordained by the Common Council of the Village of Tombstone:
>
> SEC. 1. That it shall be unlawful for any person not an officer of the law to have or carry in the Village of Tombstone any fire-arms, knife or other dangerous weapons, concealed about his person without a written permit from the Mayor, and any one violating this provision shall be fined in a sum not to exceed fifty dollars ($50), or to be confined in the village jail for thirty days, or both, in the discretion of the court.
>
> SEC. 2. When travelers, prospectors, miners, or other strangers not resident of the Village of Tombstone enter the limits of the same with any dangerous weapon upon or about their person, it shall be the duty of the Village Marshal to notify them of this ordinance and request them to dispense with those weapons, and if any one so requested neglect to refuse to comply with the same, he shall be deemed guilty of a violation of this ordinance.
>
> This ordinance shall take effect and be in force from and after its passage and publication according to law.
>
> Passed by the Common Council of the Village of Tombstone, April 12, A. D. 1880.

Tombstone Epitaph, August 14, 1880

Virgil found Ike on 4th Street, hit him over the head with his pistol, disarmed him and arrested him for carrying guns inside the city limits. While waiting for the Justice of the Peace, Morgan, Wyatt and Ike began to quarrel again. By now the Earps had grown tired of Ike's drunken threats against themselves and their friend, "Doc" Holliday. Whether it was lack of sleep, or frustration at not being able to arrest and convict the outlaws, the Earp's patience with Ike and the others was gone. Ike was fined $25.00 plus court costs, and his weapons were delivered to the Grand Hotel until he left town. Out on the street, Wyatt had an altercation with Tom McLaury, and struck him over the head. Frank McLaury and Billy Clanton arrived in Tombstone while all of this was going on. In fact "Doc" ran into the pair and politely said, "How are you?" as they entered the Grand Hotel for a drink. By now Billy Claiborne had joined the gang to take Ike and Tom to the doctor for their aching heads.

When they heard about the events of the last 18 hours, Frank and the youngest Clanton went to find their brothers and get them out of town. The Clantons, McLaurys and Billy Claiborne made their way to a vacant lot on Fremont Street between Fly's Boarding House and William Harwood's home. The Earps and "Doc" Holliday met on the corner of 4th and Allen Streets in front of Hafford's Saloon, and both groups were armed and discussing what their next steps would be. Sheriff Behan was summoned while getting his morning shave, and he approached the Earps and offered to disarm the "Cowboys" to avoid a fight. Virgil agreed to let Behan try, and they waited on that corner for word. The outlaws refused to disarm themselves as long as the Earps and Holliday remained armed. As the discussion continued, Virgil and his Special Deputies began to walk up 4th Street toward Fremont Street. Near the corner they met the empty-handed Behan claiming he had disarmed the five. Virgil clearly saw no weapons had been confiscated and they continued toward the vacant lot. Now Behan makes a very contradictory statement. He warns the Earps not to go down there or they will be murdered. How can five unarmed men kill four armed men? Behan scurried through the alley and continued to urge his companions to surrender their guns. What follows is not available in the newspaper microfilms. It is a transcription of the Daily Nugget account of the fight on Fremont Street.

A Desperate Street Fight

Marshal Virgil Earp, Morgan and Wyatt Earp and
Doc Holliday Meet the "Cowboys" – Three Men
Killed and Two Wounded, One Seriously –
Origins of the Trouble and its Tragic Termination

The 26th of October, 1881, will always be marked as one of the crimson days in the annals of Tombstone, a day when blood flowed as water, and human life was held as a shuttlecock, a day always to be remembered as witnessing the bloodiest and deadliest street fight that has ever occurred in this place, or probably in the Territory.

The origin of the trouble dates back to the first arrest of Stilwell and Spencer for the robbery of the Bisbee stage. The co-operation of the Earps and the Sheriff and his deputies in the arrest caused a number of "Cowboys" to, it is said, threaten the lives of all interested in the capture. Still, nothing occurred to indicate that any such threats would be carried into execution. But Tuesday night Ike Clanton and Doc Holliday had some difficulty in the Alhambra saloon. Hard words passed between them, and when they parted it was generally understood that the feeling between the two men was that of intense hatred. Yesterday morning Clanton came on the street armed with a rifle and revolver, but was almost immediately arrested by Marshal Earp, dismissed and fined by Justice Wallace for carrying concealed weapons. While in the Court room Wyatt Earp told him that as he had made threats against his life he wanted him to make his fight, to say how, when and where he would fight, and to get his crowd, and he (Wyatt) would be on hand.

In reply, Clanton said: "Four feet of ground is enough for me to fight on, and I'll be there." A short time after this William Clanton and Frank McLowry (sic)] came into town, and as Thomas

McLowry was already here the feeling soon became general that a fight would ensue before the day was over, and crowds of expectant men stood on the corner of Allen and Fourth streets awaiting the coming conflict.

It was now about two o'clock, and at this time Sheriff Behan appeared upon the scene and told Marshal Earp that if he disarmed his posse, composed of Morgan and Wyatt Earp, and Doc Holliday, he would go down to the O.K. Corral where Ike and James ffsic] Clanton and Frank and Tom McLowry were and disarm them. The Marshal did not desire to do this until assured that there was no danger of attack from the other party. The Sheriff went to the corral and told the "Cowboys" that they must put their arms away and not have any trouble. Ike Clanton and Tom McLowry said they were not armed, and Frank McLowry said he would not lay his aside. In the meantime the Marshal had concluded to go and, if possible, end the matter by disarming them, and as he and his posse came down Fremont Street towards the corral, the Sheriff stepped out and said: "Hold up boys, don't go down there or there will be trouble: I have been down there to disarm them." But they passed on, and when within a few feet of the Marshal said to the Clantons and McLowrys: "Throw up your hands boys, I intend to disarm you."

As he spoke, Frank McLowry made a motion to draw his revolver, when Wyatt Earp pulled his and shot him, the ball striking on the right side of his abdomen. About the same time Doc Holliday shot Tom McLowry in the right side using a short shotgun, such as is carried by Wells–Fargo & Co.'s messengers. In the meantime Billy Clanton had shot at Morgan Earp, the ball passing through the point of the left shoulder blade across the back, just grazing the backbone and coming out at the shoulder, the ball remaining inside his shirt. He fell to the ground but in an instant gathered himself, and raising in a sitting position fired at Frank McLowry as he crossed Fremont Street, and at the same instant Doc Holliday shot at him, both balls taking effect either of which would have proved fatal, as one struck him in the right temple and the other in the left breast. As he started across the street, however, he pulled his gun down on Holliday saying, "I've got you now." "Blaze away! You're a daisy if you have," replied Doc. This shot of McLowry's passed through Holliday's pistol pocket, just grazing the skin.

While this was going on Billy Clanton had shot Virgil Earp in the right leg, the ball passing through the calf, inflicting a severe flesh wound. In turn he had been shot by Morgan Earp in the right wrist and once in the left breast. Soon after the shooting commenced Ike Clanton ran through the O.K. Corral, across Allen Street into Kellogg's saloon and thence into Toughnut Street where he was arrested and taken to the county jail. The firing altogether didn't occupy more than twenty-five seconds, during which time fully thirty shots were fired. After the fight was over Billy Clanton, who, with wonderful vitality, survived his wounds for fully an hour, was carried by the editor and foreman of the Nugget into a house near where he lay, and everything possible was done to make his last moments easy. He was "game" to the last, never uttering a word of complaint, and just before breathing his last he said, "Goodbye boys; go away and let me die." The wounded were taken to their houses, and at three o'clock the next morning were resting comfortably. The dead bodies were taken in charge by the Coroner, and an inquest will be held upon them at 10 o'clock today. Upon the person of Thomas McLowry was found between $300 and $400 and checks and certificates of deposit to the amount of nearly $3,000.

During the shooting Sheriff Behan was standing nearby commanding the contestants to cease firing but was powerless to prevent it. Several parties who were in the vicinity of the shooting had "narrow escapes" from being shot. One man who had lately arrived from the east had a ball pass through his pants. He left for home this morning. A person called "the Kid" who shot Hicks at Charleston recently, was also grazed by a ball. When the Vizina [mine] whistle gave the signal that there was a conflict between the officers and "Cowboys", the mines on the hill shut down and the miners were brought to the surface. From the Contention mine a number of men, fully armed, were sent to town on a four-horse carriage. At the request of the Sheriff the "Vigilantes," or Committee of Safety, were called from the streets by a few sharp toots from the Vizina's whistle. During the early part of the evening there was a rumor that a mob would attempt to take Ike Clanton from the jail and lynch him, and to prevent any such unlawful proceedings a strong guard of deputies [fsic] was placed around that building and will be so continued until all danger is past.

At 8 o'clock last evening Finn Clanton, a brother of Billy and Ike, came to town, and placing himself under the guard of the Sheriff, visited the morgue to see the remains of his brother, and then passed the night in jail in company with the other.

OMINOUS SOUNDS

Shortly after the shooting ceased the whistle at the Vizina mine sounded a few short toots, and almost simultaneously a large number of citizens appeared on the streets armed with rifles and a belt of cartridges around their waists. These men formed in line and offered their services to the peace officers to preserve order in case any attempt at disturbance was made, or any interference offered to the authorities of the law. However, no hostile move was made by anyone, and the quiet and order was fully restored, and in a short time the excitement died away.

AT THE MORGUE

The bodies of the three slain "Cowboys" lay side by side, covered with a sheet. Very little blood appeared on their clothing, and only on the face of young Billy Clanton was there any distortion of the features or evidence of pain in dying. The features of the two McLowry boys looked as calm and placid in death as if they had died peaceably, surrounded by loving friends and sorrowing relatives. No unkind remarks were made by anyone, but feeling of unusual sorrow seemed to prevail at the sad occurrence. Of the two McLowry brothers we could learn nothing of their previous history before coming to Arizona. The two brothers owned quite an extensive ranch on the lower San Pedro, some seventy or eighty miles from this city, to which they had removed their band of cattle since the recent Mexican and Indian troubles. They did not bear the reputation of being of a quarrelsome disposition, but were known as fighting men, and have generally conducted themselves in a quiet and orderly manner when in Tombstone.

Tombstone Daily Nugget, October 27, 1881

In thirty seconds, thirty shots were fired leaving three men dead, Frank McLaury, Tom McLaury and Billy Clanton. Three men were wounded, Virgil was shot through the calf of his left leg, "Doc" was grazed on the hip and Morgan was the most seriously injured. The bullet went in his right shoulder and came out his left shoulder after nicking his spine. The main antagonist, Ike Clanton, ran away unharmed. This is significant in that is the Earp party had gone in to the vacant lot with the intent to kill all of the outlaws, Ike, Billy Claiborne and maybe even John Behan would have been dead. In 1918 Wyatt Earp drew "maps" detailing the position of the participants before and after the shooting:

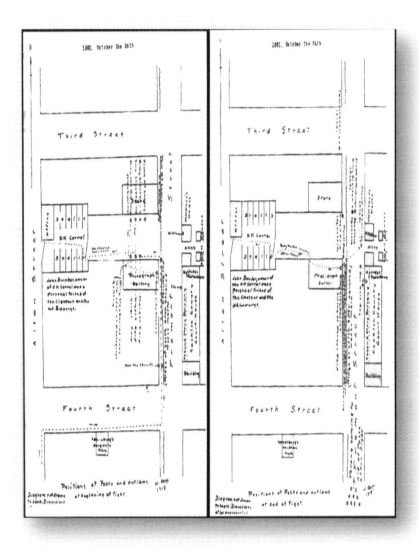

Author's Collection

Ironically that same day William Tecumseh Sherman, Commander of the Armies, sent a desperate plea to the Secretary of War, Robert Lincoln, begging for "precise orders" to enable his men to deal with the "Cowboys".

> Headquarters Army of the United States.
> Washington D.C. Oct. 26. 1881.
>
> To the Hon. R. T. Lincoln,
> Secretary of War.
> Sir:
> In considering the enclosed communication of M. de Zamacona, Mexican Minister, submitted by the Hon. Sec of State in his letter of October 20. I beg to send you several communications from Genl. Wilcox Comdg the Dept of Arizona, and on these points, and then to frame such instructions, as will enable me to give clear and precise orders to the Officers serving on that distant border, who now construe the "Posse Comitatus Law," as tying their hands.
>
> I am &c
> (Sgd) W. T. Sherman
>   General.

Letter from William T. Sherman to Robert Lincoln, October 26, 1881

Courtesy of The National Archives and Records Administration Publication Number: M2028 Publication Title: Records Relating to U.S. Marshal Crawley P. Dake, the Earp Brothers, and Lawlessness and 'Cowboy Depredations' in Arizona Territory, 1881-85. Record Group Number: 60 Record Group Title: General Records of the Department of Justice
National Archives II, College Park, Maryland

CHAPTER SEVEN

A Coroner's Inquest was held, but they could not, or would not, make a determination whether the killings were justified, and most importantly, if the City Marshal and Deputies were merely performing their duties as officers of the law. The Earps and "Doc" Holliday would be forced to endure a judicial inquest to determine if charges of murder would be filed against them. This action in Judge Spicer's court would last for thirty days. Here two interesting points should be noted. First, Wells Spicer was the U.S. Commissioner of Courts, or Federal Judge for the district, and Virgil was the U.S. Deputy Marshal in the same district. Secondly, Frank & Tom McLaury's brother, William, was an attorney in Fort Worth, Texas. Will journeyed to Tombstone and assisted the prosecution against the Earps and Holliday. Yet no objections before during or after the inquest were made by any party in reference to any conflict of interest. After the Daily Nugget newspaper ignored Judge Spicer's "gag" order, the testimony was published daily by both papers. The Tombstone Epitaph had joined the newly created Associated Press, so John Clum's accounts of the plight in Cochise County had been broadcast throughout the country. Tombstone was abuzz with gossip for and against both sides. Nationally, the gunfight brought the territory's struggle to subdue the "Cowboys" into the spotlight. U.S. Marshal Crawley Dake became suddenly mute, as did Washington, D.C. The politicos chose to defer further action until a ruling was made whether murder charges would be filed.

It is certain that Virgil felt abandoned by the City and Federal Governments. He was removed as City Marshal pending the outcome of the inquest, and his Federal superiors were incommunicado. Not the entire world remained silent. The following article was reprinted in the Daily Epitaph from the San Francisco Daily Report:

Tombstone Epitaph, November 19, 1881

Judge Wells Spicer ruled on November 30, 1881 that the Earps and Holliday had acted within the boundaries of their duties as lawmen. He admonished Virgil for his selection of Deputies, but empathized with his choices under the circumstances. The Nugget carried this editorial the next day:

Tombstone Daily Nugget, December 1, 1881

The ruling did not bring finality to the state of affairs. Ike Clanton would attempt to indict the four on Contention City for the killings. But this would be dismissed as already ruled upon. As Will McLaury left Tombstone for his home and practice in Fort Worth, he put a $1,000.00 bounty out for the death of each of the Earps and Holliday.

U.S. Marshal Crawley Dake finally notified Washington, D.C. of the street fight in Tombstone on December 3, 1881. Five days later, Dake would send a telegram outlining the same details, which on its face is very strange. Today the U.S. Marshal Service states there is no proof any Earp brother was <u>ever</u> a U.S. Deputy Marshal. In the late 1920's, Billy Breakenridge and John Clum both published books about Tombstone, and they each, independently, said Wyatt was a U.S. Deputy Marshal <u>before</u> he came to Tombstone. The lack of provenance is due to the fact that Crawley Dake kept few if any records as U.S. Marshal of the Arizona Territory. In 1885, Mr. Dake was investigated for embezzlement because his wife acquired nearly $23,000.00 worth of property in Prescott, A.T. during his tenure as U.S. Marshal. Even then Dake stated that as far as he was concerned, Wyatt was still a U.S. Deputy Marshal.

OFFICE OF
UNITED STATES MARSHAL,
TERRITORY OF ARIZONA.

C. P. DAKE, Marshal.

Prescott, Arizona, December 3rd, 1881.

Hon. S. F. Phillips.
Acting Attorney General.
Washington D.C.

Sir,

In reply to your favor of the 17th ultimo, from Secretary Blaine &c. with enclosures, I have the honor to report as follows:—

I do not know of any rivalry between the United States officers and the County officials of Tombstone or elsewhere, that in any way interferes or retards my deputies from bringing to justice outlaws or "Cow boys" so called:—

'Tis true, the Sheriff of Cochise County, (bordering on Sonora,) in which Tombstone is situated, attempted to interfere with the Messrs Earp and their assistants but the attempt has completely failed.— The Earps have rid Tombstone and neighborhood of the presence of this outlaw element.— They killed several Cow boys in Tombstone recently— and the Sheriff's faction had my deputies arrested— and after a

OFFICE OF
UNITED STATES MARSHAL,
TERRITORY OF ARIZONA.

C. P. DAKE Marshal

Prescott, Arizona 188

protracted trial my deputies were vindicated and publicly complimented for their bravery in driving this outlaw element from this part of our Territory. The magistrate discharged my deputies on the ground that when they killed Clanton, and the McLowry's, they were in the legitimate discharge of their duties as my officers.

Hereafter my deputies will not be interfered with in hunting down Stage Robbers, Mail Robbers, Train Robbers, Cattle thieves, and all that class of murdering banditti on the border.

I am proud to report that I have some of the best and bravest men in my employ in this hazardous business — men who are trusty and tried, and who strike fear into the hearts of these outlaws.

In conclusion I beg leave to state that I am fully able to grapple with this outlaw element, having this force of deputies at my command. Yet the expense you must doubtless perceive is great. Therefore, if you will make a

OFFICE OF
UNITED STATES MARSHAL,
TERRITORY OF ARIZONA.

C. P. DAKE Marshal

Prescott, Arizona _____ 188__

special appropriation for this purpose, only for such an amount (as you may deem fit, the premises considered,) I will put this element out of the way and drive them from our borders, as was done with the revolutionists under Marquez. The existing fees allowed by law are insufficient to induce men to risk their lives in this business. They must be allowed living fees, such as are allowed by our Territorial Laws to Sheriffs for such services, and mileage. I will promptly send on the vouchers for your approval as they accrue, and will keep close attention to the expense list, and will be as economical in this matter as I possibly can.

I enclose herewith, clippings, to show how the Press support my deputies, — also a letter from Gov. Gosper who has recently returned from the border.

Very respectfully
Your obedient servant
C. P. Dake
U. S. Marshal

Courtesy of The National Archives and Records Administration Publication Number: M2028 Publication Title: Records Relating to U.S. Marshal Crawley P. Dake, the Earp Brothers, and Lawlessness and 'Cowboy Depredations' in Arizona Territory, 1881-85. Record Group Number: 60 Record Group Title: General Records of the Department of Justice
National Archives II, College Park, Maryland

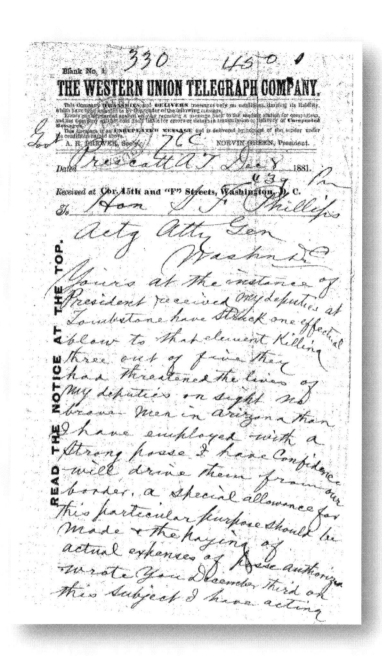

Courtesy of The National Archives and Records Administration Publication Number: M2028 Publication Title: Records Relating to U.S. Marshal Crawley P. Dake, the Earp Brothers, and Lawlessness and 'Cowboy Depredations' in Arizona Territory, 1881-85. Record Group Number: 60 Record Group Title: General Records of the Department of Justice
National Archives II, College Park, Maryland

The importance of these two documents lies in their plurality, literally. Both messages refer to "my **deputies**;" "no braver **men** have I had in my employ;" "the **Earps**;" "**they**;" etc. Although they may appear to have been possible mistakes, they are significant. These two communiqués imply that all of the Earp brothers were U.S. Deputy Marshals acting under the authority of Crawley Dake at the time of the gunfight.

With the Earp party exonerated for the deaths of Billy Clanton and the McLaury boys, the cry for action reached the White House. In his first address to Congress, December 6, 1881, President Chester A. Arthur took on this controversial issue:

The Acting Attorney-General also calls attention to the disturbance of the public tranquillity during the past year in the Territory of Arizona. A band of armed desperadoes known as "Cowboys," probably numbering from fifty to one hundred men, have been engaged for months in committing acts of lawlessness and brutality which the local authorities have been unable to repress. The depredations of these "Cowboys" have also extended into Mexico, which the marauders reach from the Arizona frontier. With every disposition to meet the exigencies of the case, I am embarrassed by lack of authority to deal with them effectually. The punishment of crimes committed within Arizona should ordinarily, of course, be left to the Territorial authorities; but it is worthy consideration whether acts which necessarily tend to embroil the United States with neighboring governments should not be declared crimes against the United States. Some of the incursions alluded to may perhaps be within the scope of the law (U. S. Revised Statutes, sec. 5286) forbidding "military expeditions or enterprises" against friendly states; but in view of the speedy assembling of your body I have preferred to await such legislation as in your wisdom the occasion may seem to demand.

It may perhaps be thought proper to provide that the setting on foot within our own territory of brigandage and armed marauding expeditions against friendly nations and their citizens shall be punishable as an offense against the United States.

I will add that in the event of a request from the Territorial government for protection by the United States against "domestic violence" this Government would be powerless to render assistance.

The act of 1795, chapter 36, passed at a time when Territorial governments received little attention from Congress, enforced this duty of the United States only as to the State governments. But the act of 1807, chapter 39, applied also to Territories. This law seems to have remained in force until the revision of the statutes, when the provision for the Territories was dropped. I am not advised whether this alteration was intentional or accidental; but as it seems to me that the Territories should be offered the protection which is accorded to the States by the Constitution, I suggest legislation to that end.

It seems to me, too, that whatever views may prevail as to the policy of recent legislation by which the Army has ceased to be a part of the *posse comitatus*, an exception might well be made for permitting the military to assist the civil Territorial authorities in enforcing the laws of the United States. This use of the Army would not seem to be within the alleged evil against which that legislation was aimed. From sparseness of population and other circumstances it is often quite impracticable to summon a civil posse in places where officers of justice require assistance and where a military force is within easy reach.

The report of the Secretary of the Interior, with accompanying documents, presents an elaborate account of the business of that Department. A summary of it would be too extended for this place. I ask your careful attention to the report itself.

Messages and Papers of the Presidents 1789-1897, Vol. VIII
By James Richardson

In spite of the publicity, the "Cowboys" would take up Will McLaury's challenge, however after the gunfight; they would revert to their normal method of attack, ambush. On December 28, 1881 as Virgil walked down Allen Street across 5th Street from the Oriental Saloon to the Crystal Palace Saloon, would be assassins let go several shotgun blasts that peppered his left side and the Crystal Palace with buckshot. Doctors were forced to remove six inches of bone from his left arm, which Virgil would never be able to use for the rest of his life. Immediately Wyatt contacted Crawley Dake, and this blurb appeared in the January 3rd Tombstone Nugget:

> Wyatt Earp has received the appointment of Deputy United States Marshal, vice Virgil Earp. Marshal Dake telegraphed the appointment upon receipt of the news of Virgil's injuries. So says the Phenix Gazette.

Tombstone Daily Nugget, January 3, 1882

Things were about to change in and around Tombstone. Wyatt Earp had officially replaced Virgil as U.S. Deputy Marshal in the area. He would surround himself with men he could trust and count on in a fight in order to bring the "Cowboys" to justice. No court had been able to convict any of the outlaws to date. Wyatt hoped to change this by bringing the fight to them. A new and old ally came to Wyatt's aid, Wells Fargo & Company. Crawley Dake could not obtain additional funding from the Department of Justice until he reconciled his existing accounts. Dake went to San Francisco to meet John Valentine, General Superintendent of Wells Fargo & Co. Whether Wyatt suggested this move is not known, but the end result was $3,000.00 from Wells Fargo & Company for use by Wyatt and his deputies.

CHAPTER EIGHT

As a U.S. Deputy Marshal for Southeastern Arizona Territory, Wyatt Earp was now more committed in the pursuit and arrest of the "Cowboys". They had disabled his older brother for life, and it appears that he was intent on making their lives a living Hell also. Wyatt put into practice the same techniques he had used in the Kansas cow towns. He and his posse searched Charleston, Benson, the San Pedro Valley, the Sulphur Springs Valley; they went into the "Cowboys" backyard, so to speak, for the men they had warrants for. Despite the higher level of intensity, the conviction rate of the "Cowboys" remained nil. His approach further divided the citizens of Tombstone. The loudest outcry came from those who profited from the outlaws' offenses. The split amongst the township began to take on political overtones. The "Cowboys" were Southern Democrats, supported by the Democratically biased Tombstone Daily Nugget newspaper, while the Earps, primarily Northern Republicans, backed by the Republican oriented Tombstone Daily Epitaph. Another factor was the Earps represented the corporate interests like Wells Fargo & company; the mining magnates; and land speculators, while the "Cowboys" represented the butchers; meat suppliers and ranchers. In the simplest of terms, it was white-collar versus blue-collar.

Each group had its own voice in Prescott and in Washington, D.C. Wyatt's more aggressive approach began to draw closer scrutiny after the increase of violence in the City Limits. January 17, 1882, was the date Tombstone almost had a fight to rival the one less than ninety days earlier. John Ringo and "Doc" Holliday came perilously close to a gun battle in the middle of a busy street. The cause of the dispute was never determined, but both men were restrained and separated. Wyatt seemed damned if he did and more damned if he didn't. The dissent reached a climax on February 2nd when the Tombstone Epitaph published the following:

DRAW YOUR OWN INFERENCE

Resignation of Virgil W. and Wyatt S. Earp as Deputy Marshals.

Below will be found the resignation of Virgil and Wyatt Earp, as deputy United States marshals. The document is a manly and generous one, and should meet with impartial criticism from the public. The position of deputy marshal on the frontier is no sinecure. An officer who honestly tries to do his duty encounters many perils that the public know not of, and raises within the breasts of criminals that desire for their death that comes from fear of the gallows and imprisonment. It would be as much out of place for a public journal, under the attendant circumstances, to endeavor to create public opinion upon these resignations, as to prejudge a case at court. It is sufficient that the matter is before the United States marshal, who has had ample opportunity to investigate the condition of affairs, and who will give the subject that deliberate and careful consideration that comes of experience in official life. The following is a copy of the resignation tendered:

TOMBSTONE, February 1, 1882.
Major C. P. Dake, United States Marshal, Grand Hotel, Tombstone—Dear Sir: In exercising our official functions as deputy United States marshals in this territory, we have endeavored always unflinchingly to perform the duties intrusted to us. These duties have been exacting and perilous in their character, having to be performed in a community where turbulence and violence could at almost any moment be organized to thwart and resist the enforcement of the processes of the court issued to bring criminals to justice. And while we have a deep sense of obligation to many of the citizens for their hearty co-operation in aiding us to suppress lawlessness, and their faith in our honesty of purpose, we realize that, notwithstanding our best efforts and judgment in everything which we have been required to perform, there has arisen so much harsh criticism in relation to our operations, and such a persistent effort having been made to misrepresent and misinterpret our acts, we are led to the conclusion that, in order to convince the public that it is our sincere purpose to promote the public welfare independent of any personal emolument or advantages to ourselves, it is our duty to place our resignations as deputy United States marshals in your hands, which we now do, thanking you for your continued courtesy and confidence in our integrity, and shall remain subject to your orders in the performance of any duties which may be assigned to us, only until our successors are appointed.

Very respectfully yours,
VIRGIL W. EARP,
WYATT S. EARP.

Tombstone Daily Epitaph, February 2, 1882

By resigning, the Earps put pressure directly on Crawley Dake. On February 4, 1882 Dake paid his "Ex" Deputies and Tombstone a visit:

> United States Marshal Dake departed for Prescott yesterday. During his brief sojourn in Tombstone he has exhibited great interest in our local affairs, and shown a disposition to contribute all in his power toward a speedy adjustment of the differences which have for some time past prevailed in this community. The Nugget feels justified in stating the Marshal secured the good-will of a majority of our citizens during his stay here.

Tombstone Daily Nugget, February 4, 1882

Based upon the content, the visit was purely political. Dake had come to Tombstone to smooth all of the ruffled feathers, the Earps and those of the town's people. He even went so far as to appoint a new U.S. Deputy Marshal, John Jackson. However, Dake never accepted the Earps' resignation. It was an advantageous and sly move on Dake's part. He now had two Deputies in Tombstone that were beyond reproach, and whose bravery could not be questioned. The new Territorial Governor, Frederick A. Tritle, felt equally confident about John Jackson's abilities and intended to name him "Captain" of a new law enforcement militia he chose to call the Arizona Rangers. More detail will come later on Tritle's efforts to field the Rangers. Wyatt and his posse remained steadfast in their efforts to end the "Cowboys'" reign of terror in Cochise County.

> **"Once More to the Breach."**
> Wyatt and Morgan Earp, Doc Holliday, "Texas Jack,' ――― Smith, McMasters, and one or two others left the city yesterday afternoon for ――― where, no one apparently knows, but when in the vicinity of Waterville they separated, four of the party going in the direction of San Simon Valley, to arrest, 'it is claimed, Pony Dehl and one or two other well known characters, and the remainder to Charleston. It is supposed they are acting in the capacity of U. S. Deputy Marshals, their resignations not having been accepted or their appointment revoked by U. S. Marshal Dake, as was generally supposed some time ago.

Tombstone Daily Nugget, February 18, 1882

The drama continued for another month. On the 18th of March, 1882, after attending the play "Stolen Kisses" performed by the Lingard troupe at Schieffelin Hall, Wyatt watched Morgan play pool at Campbell & Hatch's Saloon on Allen Street. Pistol shots exploded through the glass panes of the back door striking Morgan through the spine and hitting the wall six inches above Wyatt's head. With one brother dead and the other permanently disabled, Wyatt's world and the history of Tombstone would be changed forever.

> His body was placed in a casket, and sent to his parents at Colton, Cal., for burial, being guarded to Contention by his brothers and two or three of his most intimate friends. The funeral cortege started away from the Cosmopolitan hotel about 12:30 yesterday, with the fire bell tolling out its solemn peals of "Earth to earth, dust to dust."

Tombstone Weekly Epitaph, February 27, 1882

The Weekly Epitaph was a compilation of the Daily issues. Unfortunately the Daily issues on microfilm are incomplete for this week, so specific dates of the events cannot be verified. In that same Weekly edition appeared the following article about Virgil's departure from Tombstone.

> V. W. Earp and wife left for his parents' home at Colton, California, to-day. He was accompanied to Contention by his brothers and several personal friends.

Tombstone Weekly Epitaph, February 27, 1882

Wyatt, his youngest brother Warren, "Doc" Holliday, "Texas Jack" Vermillion, "Turkey Creek" Jack Johnson, Sherman McMasters and possibly O.C. Smith and Dan Tipton were probably the members of the "funeral cortege." We do have this item from March 24, 1882:

> Mrs. James Earp and Mrs. Wyatt Earp left to-day for Colton, California, the residence of their husbands' parents. These ladies have the sympathy of all who know them, and for that matter the entire community. Their trials for the last six months have been of the most severe nature.

Tombstone Daily Epitaph, March 24, 1882

Looking at these bits and pieces, no article mentions James, the oldest Earp brother. Conventional thinking has always placed Wyatt and his posse escorting Morgan's body along with the rest of the family in Tombstone to the railhead in Contention and then on to Tucson. But based on the fact that Bessie and Mattie left without an entourage or protection indicates that James took Morgan's body on to Colton from Contention City, and that the posse accompanied Virgil and Allie all the way to Tucson.

CHAPTER NINE

On the night of March 20, 1882, the saga between the Earp brothers and the "Cowboys" would take a significant turn, a turn that would catapult the Earps' 28-month residency in Tombstone, Arizona Territory in to romantic legend. Wyatt, his posse with Virgil and Allie arrived at the Tucson train station and had dinner at the adjoining hotel. J.W. Evans, the U.S. Deputy Marshal in Tucson told Wyatt that Ike Clanton, Frank Stillwell and maybe more "Cowboys" had been seen lingering around the train yard. The posse quickly spread out to look for the outlaws knowing that all of their lives were in danger. Wyatt found Stilwell and pulled both triggers on his sawed-off 10 gauge shotgun nearly cutting Stilwell in two. Several additional pistol wounds were found on the body the next day. But the first man named in the Coroner's Inquest on Morgan's murder was dead.

ANOTHER KILLING

This Time the Thunderbolt of Death Strikes the Other Side

The people of Tombstone were startled this morning with a report from Tucson that Frank Stilwell, a well known personage in this county as late deputy sheriff at Bisbee and as one of the alleged Bisbee stage robbers, as also suspected of having killed an old man at the Bronkow mine some two or three years ago, had been found dead from the effects of a charge of buckshot near the Porter house, at the depot in Tucson. By a special dispatch to the EPITAPH, in another column, the report is confirmed and the full particulars given, so far as at present known. The dispatch is in error when it states that the remains of Morgan Earp were on the train. It should have been that Virgil W. Earp and wife were on the train, they having left Tombstone for Colton yesterday.

As the dispatch says, there are two theories of the killing here as at Tucson. One is, that the comrades of Stilwell, fearing that he might turn states evidence, have silenced him; and others that it is the work of the incensed Earp brothers for the assassination of Morgan, it being stated that there is positive evidence that Stilwell was in Tombstone Saturday night at the time Morgan Earp was murdered, and that he rode into Tucson on horseback on Sunday. In either case his taking off verifies the saying that "the way of the transgressor is hard."

Tombstone Weekly Epitaph, March 27, 1882

The Stilwell Assassination.

The assassination of Frank Stilwell in Tucson Monday night was, there is little doubt, but another act in the bitter faction feud which has worked untold harm to the interests of Tombstone and Cochise County during the past six months. As all well-informed persons were satisfied that the killing of Morgan Earp in this city Saturday night was the natural and legitimate sequence of preceding acts of violence, so, in regard to this latter assassination, everybody conversant with the facts is equally well satisfied that it was but the natural outgrowth of the same causes. And as all right-thinking and order-loving citizens denounced and deprecated the unlawful killing of Earp, so will the murder of Stilwell, which surrounded by all the cowardly fiendishness of the former, create a feeling of loathing for the perpetrators and horror at the deed in the breasts of every man possessed of the common instincts of humanity or any regard for the preservation of organized society. The NUGGET condemned in words of no uncertain meaning the dastardly act of Saturday night, and it now denounces the red-handed assassins of Stilwell, and places them in the same category as the skulking murderers of Earp. It is to be earnestly hoped the cowardly perpetrators of two of the foulest, ghoul-like assassinations that ever disgraced any community, may be speedily identified, that justice stern and unrelenting may be swiftly meted out to them.

Tombstone Daily Nugget, March 22, 1882

The violence of Cochise County had now reached over the Pima County Line. The citizens of both counties were shocked. Pima County issued a warrant for the arrest of Wyatt and his posse for murder almost immediately. This news was telegraphed to Sheriff Behan in Tombstone, which set up what has become a classic confrontation in the Old West.

WOULD NOT BE ARRESTED.

The Earp Party Refuse to be Arrested by Sheriff Behan, and Leave The City.

Sheriff Behan yesterday received a telegram from the authorities at Tucson, requesting him to arrest Wyatt Earp, Doc. Holliday, Sherman McMasters and one Johnson, and hold them until further advices. Shortly after the receipt of the telegram, Sheriff Behan went to the Cosmopolitan Hotel, where he found the two Earp brothers, Wyatt and Warren, Holliday, Texas Jack, Johnson and McMasters. The Sheriff informed the party of his mission, when, in an instant, each one leveled a sixshooter at the officer, and peremptorily refused to submit to arrest. The Sheriff retired, and immediately took measures to raise a posse to enable him to accomplish his duty.

SCORES OF VOLUNTEERS

proffered their services to aid in the enforcement of the law, and arms for a sufficient number were quickly obtained from the store of P. W. Smith & Co. Immediately upon the enforced retirement of the Sheriff from the hotel, the Earp party, six in number, also left the premises, all heavily armed, and betook themselves to the corral, corner of Allen and Third streets, where their horses were, ready saddled, and quickly mounting, they rode rapidly out of town, in the direction of Contention. The Sheriff, finding that the time consumed in arming and equipping his posse had enabled the other party to secure at least half an hour's start, concluded not to commence the pursuit until this morning at 5 o'clock.

The destination of the Earp party is of course unknown. Many are of the opinion that they have gone direct to Tucson, with the intention of giving themselves up to Sheriff Paul. Others, among whom is Chief of Police Neagle, are very emphatic in the belief that the fugitives will avoid the ancient pueblo of Pima county as long as possible, giving as a reason for this belief that strong evidence is in the hands of the Tucson officials implicating the parties "wanted" in the assassination of Stilwell.

The action of Sheriff Behan in attempting the arrest before completing his preparations to enforce it if necessary, was strongly censured last night by many of our citizens. The Sheriff certainly has as good cause as any in this community to know the desperate character of the men with whom he had to deal, and it is possible he was a little hasty or over-confident in the authority vested in him.

Tombstone Daily Nugget, March 23, 1882

Wyatt and his posse moved quickly away from Tombstone. On March 22, 1882 they arrived at Pete Spence's ranch and wood camp. Here they found Florentine Cruz, a.k.a. "Indian Charlie," who was also named in Morgan's Coroner's Inquest. Cruz was killed trying to escape Wyatt and his men. Then the group seemed to disappear again.

> **More About the Earps.**
>
> TUCSON, March 24.—Nothing more has been heard from the Earp party since their killing the Mixican, Florentino, in the Dragoon Mountains. It is reported on good authority that they propose to kill three more men who they believe were a party to the killing of their brother, then they will leave the country or surrender. Two posses are after them—Sheriff Behan, of Cochise county, with eighteen men, and a party of cowboys from Charleston, numbering twenty-one. If they are overtaken a terrible fight will ensue. It is believed that they will elude their pursuers and return to Tombstone any hour and attempt the murder of Pete Spence, who has been arrested on suspicion. Parties just in from Tombstone say Spence is in jail and has been armed so as to defend himself if an attempt is made by the Earps.

Tombstone Daily Nugget, March 25, 1882

Wyatt arranged to have O.C. Smith bring much needed money to Iron Springs in the Whetstone Mountains, but there was already a group camping at the springs. On March 24, 1882, they rode in on the men camping at the springs, and discovered it was "Curly Bill" Brocius and several other "Cowboys". The firefight was reported that same day:

BATTLE OF BURLEIGH.

Two Versions of the Fight.

You Pays Your Money and You Takes Your Choice.

In the account of the battle of Burleigh, given in Saturday's EPITAPH, the facts were faithfully given to our reporter, and upon later inquiries being made it is asserted upon what is considered good authority that it was correct in all essential points other than the locality, which, it is stated, was purposely misrepresented. It has since been learned that in the fire of the cowboys that Wyatt Earp received seven shots through his clothes, but was not scratched by a bullet, and that one shot went through McMasters' clothes, just creasing his person, but doing no serious damage whatever. The horse of Texas Jack was shot dead and the pommel of one of the saddles was shot off, which completes the list of casualties to the Earp party, so far as can be learned. It is still asserted that

CURLY BILL WAS KILLED

upon the return fire of the new-comers at the spring. His death is stoutly denied by the cowboy party, however, who say that he is not in this part of the country, while the other side as positively assert its truth. It would seem that the Earp party, every man of whom knows Curly Bill as well as they would their own reflections in a glass, ought to know whether it was him or his double, if he has one.

THE COWBOY VERSION.

On Friday last, Dick Wright, better known in Tombstone as "Whistling Dick," and Tony Kraker, were out on the mesa west of Drew's ranch, below Contention, in search of strayed mules, and just at evening they rode down to the spring when they were suddenly confronted by four men with leveled guns pointed directly at them. Tony sung out, "what are you doing there, you lop-eared Missourian?" This original salutation disarmed the cowboys, who lowered their guns and invited Tony and Dick to get down and make themselves at home, which they did. Sitting around the camp fire the four cowboys told them their version of the story, which was as follows: They said that they were camped at the spring, when they saw the Earp party ride down, and not knowing how they stood with them, they thought that they would

GIVE THEM A SHOT

just for luck, so they blazed away and shot off the pommel of Wyatt Earp's saddle and killed the horse that Texas Jack was riding. They said that not one of the Earp party charged upon them, but Wyatt, the balance all running away. Wyatt dismounted and fired his gun at them but without effect. Texas Jack is said to have jumped up behind one of the other boys a la Mexicana, and off they went as rapidly as they could. These are about as near the two sides of the fight as can be got at at this time.

A LUDICROUS SCENE.

The other side, who claim to have killed Curly Bill and remained masters of the situation, say that after the battle was over and they had returned to their horses, and Texas Jack had found his beautiful pony dead; one that had carried him from Texas to Tombstone, and over many a weary and scorching plain in Texas, New Mexico and Arizona, knelt down by the side of the faithful beast, unharped his angered brow, and there, upon his bended knees, took a deep and desperate oath to avenge the poor animal's death. This incident aptly illustrates the old saying that, "It is but a step from the sublime to the ridiculous."

With the foregoing statements the reader will be able to draw some conclusion that may satisfy his or her mind about the late battle of so-called Burleigh.

Tombstone Daily Epitaph, March 24, 1882

As previously stated, the confrontation between Wyatt, "Curly Bill" and the others actually occurred at Irons Springs in the Whetstone Mountains. This report may have been an attempt by the Epitaph to throw off Behan and his "posse." In less than four whole days, three of the men thought to be involved in the planning or perpetration of Morgan Earp's murder had themselves been dispatched by U.S. Deputy Marshal Wyatt Earp and his posse of Federal assistants. At Iron Springs, "Texas Jack" Vermillion's horse had been killed, so Wyatt directed the men north to Graham County. Here they found sanctuary at Henry Hooker's ranch, the Sierra Bonita.

**Photograph of the Sierra Bonita Ranch, circa 1880's
Courtesy of Tim Fattig**

Hooker tried to give Wyatt the $1,000.00 bounty the Cattleman's Association had offered for "Curly Bill," but Wyatt refused. He did ask Hooker if he would consider replacing Vermillion's horse instead, and Henry Hooker agreed. Wyatt also said he was expecting $1,000.00 to be delivered by E.B. Gage, the General Superintendent of the Grand Central Mine. This is very curious, because Gage had been a staunch supporter of the Earps, but at that time he was not known to be one of the big "players" in Tombstone yet. Perhaps he was a messenger for the corporate consortium in

Tombstone, and they were helping supply the funds to the band.

The ultimate confrontation nearly took place not far from Hooker's ranch. It seems Wyatt was warned that Behan and his "posse" were headed for the ranch. He and his men set up camp on top of a hill about three miles from the ranch house. Behan's first arrival at the ranch almost caused a fight between the "posse" and Hooker's ranch hands, but cooler heads prevailed. Sheriff Behan then went to Fort Grant to secure scouts, but was refused the use of any Army personnel. He then returned to the Sierra Bonita and was advised that Wyatt and his men had been waiting for Behan and his "posse" on the nearby hill. It was at this point that John Behan made the astute observation that he was out of his jurisdiction and returned to Tombstone empty-handed. Wyatt knew better than to wait too long, and he led his men in to New Mexico Territory. While on Hooker's ranch, one of Wyatt's men sent a letter to the Epitaph, which is included in this "summary-of-events" article:

Tombstone Daily Epitaph, April 5, 1882

April 1, 1882, John Thacker, Wells Fargo & Co. agent, sent a letter to John Valentine, the General Superintendent for the company, requesting that he use his considerable political influence to get Governor Tritle's legislation passed. Governor Tritle had drafted legislation requesting two key amendments to the Arizona Territorial Statutes. The first removed the ambiguity, as Tritle called it, of the law regarding the Governor's power to remove/replace county officials for corruption, dereliction of duty, etc. Through this change Tritle could remove Behan and replace for six months, or until a General Election. The second appropriated $150,000.00 in Federal funds to create and field the Arizona Rangers, a Territorial Law Enforcement unit modeled after the Texas Rangers. In all of his correspondence to Washington, D.C., Governor Tritle never mentions Behan by name. However, John Thacker specifically names him as the target of the proposal. Unfortunately the letters that follow have sustained water damage, but the message is very clear.

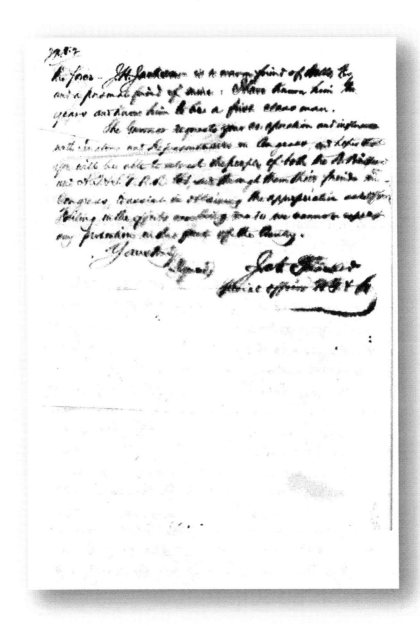

Letter from John Thacker to John Valentine, April 1, 1882

Courtesy of The National Archives and Records Administration Publication Number: M2028 Publication Title: Records Relating to U.S. Marshal Crawley P. Dake, the Earp Brothers, and Lawlessness and 'Cowboy Depredations' in Arizona Territory, 1881-85. Record

Group Number: 60 Record Group Title: General Records of the Department of Justice
National Archives II, College Park, Maryland

Lloyd Tevis, the President of Wells Fargo & Company sent the following letter to his political contacts in an effort to pass the legislation.

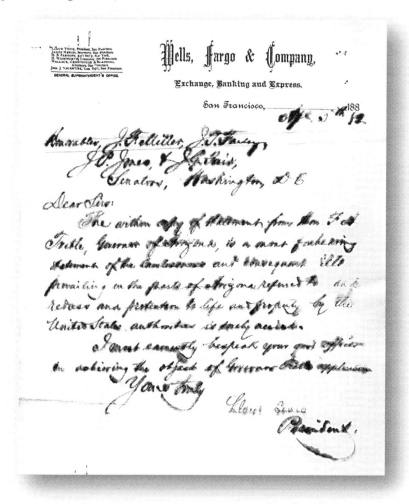

Letter from Lloyd Tevis to U.S. Senators

Courtesy of The National Archives and Records Administration Publication Number: M2028 Publication Title: Records Relating to U.S. Marshal Crawley P. Dake, the Earp Brothers, and Lawlessness

and 'Cowboy Depredations' in Arizona Territory, 1881-85. Record Group Number: 60 Record Group Title: General Records of the Department of Justice
National Archives II, College Park, Maryland

President Arthur had a different idea, and his proposed legislation, including deleted paragraphs, follows:

> On the ground of economy, as well as effectiveness, however, it appears to me to be more advisable to permit the co-operation with the civil authorities of a part of the Army as a <u>posse comitatus</u>. Believing that this, in addition to such use of the Army as may be made under the powers already conferred by section 5298 Rev. Stat., would be adequate to secure the accomplishment of the ends in view, I again call the attention of Congress to the expediency of so amending section 15 of the act of June 18, 1878, chap. 263, as to allow the military forces to be employed as a <u>posse comitatus</u> to assist the civil authorities within a Territory to execute the laws therein. This use of the Army, as I have in my former message observed, would not seem to be within the alleged evil against which that legislation was aimed. I submit herewith the form of an amendment, which indicates the additional legislation deemed by me to be needed, and I recommend the adoption of a provision corresponding thereto in terms or substance.
>
> That Section 15 of the act of June 18, 1878, chapter 263, be amended by adding thereto the following words: "<u>Provided</u>, That the President may, where in his judgment the civil authorities of and within any Territory cannot by the ordinary means at their command execute the laws, authorize the employment of the military forces of the United States as a <u>posse comitatus</u> for that purpose."

President Arthur's Amendment Proposal, April 26, 1882

Courtesy of The National Archives and Records Administration Publication Number: M2028 Publication Title: Records Relating to U.S. Marshal Crawley P. Dake, the Earp Brothers, and Lawlessness and 'Cowboy Depredations' in Arizona Territory, 1881-85. Record Group Number: 60 Record Group Title: General Records of the Department of Justice
National Archives II, College Park, Maryland

Wyatt Earp, Warren Earp, John H. "Doc" Holliday, "Texas Jack" Vermillion, "Turkey Creek" Jack Johnson, Sherman McMasters, O.C. Smith and Dan Tipton reached Silver City, New Mexico on April 15, 1882. From here they moved northward to their ultimate destination, Colorado, where Wyatt's good friend Bat Masterson was a lawman. Yet during this journey, the Epitaph printed two articles, which may have been intended to mask the Earp Posse's exit and still keep the fear of the unknown in the Cowboys.

> It is reported that the Earp party have been employed by the authorities of New Mexico to hunt down and arrest the parties who are known to have been interested in the massacre of the Mexicans at Skull canyon, New Mexico, last summer. This may account for the report in the Nugget this morning that they were seen to board the train at Deming and go east.

Tombstone Daily Epitaph, April 20, 1882

The Earps.

It has been learned from reliable authority that the Earp party sold their entire outfit in Silver City, New Mexico, and came down to Deming on the 17th inst., where they bought tickets over the Atchison, Topeka & Santa Fe road, and took the train east. It is believed that this action on their part is a confirmation of the report of yesterday that they have gone to the aid of the New Mexico authorities in bringing to justice the parties who are known to have been in the massacre of the Mexicans at Skull canyon, New Mexico, last summer. In their capacity of detectives, it is said that the Earps have full knowledge of every person concerned in that damnable affair, and that this fact having come to the knowledge of the authorities of New Mexico, they have decided to make an effort to bring the whole gang to justice. If the Earps have left the country this is the most probable theory of the cause and their destination.

Tombstone Daily Epitaph, April 21, 1882

While in Albuquerque, New Mexico Territory, Wyatt gave an interview to the Evening Review newspaper. It was published after he and his men left town, but it contains an interesting point:

HE STATED HE HAD COME TO ALBUQUERQUE TO ESCAPE PROSECUTION WHILE AWAITING THE RESULT OF AN EFFORT BEING MADE BY GOVERNOR TRITLE TO SECURE THEIR PARDON FROM THE PRESIDENT;

Albuquerque Evening Review, My 13, 1882

The reporter went on to add that Wyatt presented "convincing documents" which supported his story. However, they did not provide any further detail on the "convincing documents." There was a perfunctory attempt to extradite "Doc" Holliday, but the Governor of Colorado failed to recognize the order from Arizona Territory. Sometime later the murder warrant for the group would be quashed. On May 3, 1882, President Chester Arthur issued the Presidential Proclamation, which preceded a declaration of martial law, demanding that the Cowboys disperse and lead normal lives. The local newspapers carried on for days with indignant editorials regarding the Proclamation, but soon the furor would subside.

On the morning of July 14, 1882, a body was discovered under a triple-trunk oak tree along West Turkey Creek in the foothills of the Chiricahua Mountains. It was John Ringo, the last of the Cowboy leaders. His death would lead to additional speculation and doubt amongst the outlaws. Ringo was found with a bullet hole in his right temple, and a huge exit wound out the top of his head. His hat was on his head, but there was no hole in the hat. Ringo's horse and boots were missing, and his undershirt was wrapped around his feet. His pistol was in his right hand, with his watch chain wrapped around the barrel. John Ringo's rifle cartridge belt was on his waist right-side up, but his pistol belt was upside down. The Coroner's Inquest simply lists the cause of death as "gunshot wound to the head" with no determination as to murder or suicide.

CHAPTER TEN

The twenty-eight months that the Earp brothers lived in Tombstone is surrounded by controversy, contradiction and conundrum. Over the years many of the local records have been destroyed or disappeared into public and private collections all over the world. There are many items that do not make sense. First let's look at the office of the U.S. Deputy Marshal in Tombstone. In the late 1920's both William Breakenridge, a Deputy for John Behan, and John Clum both published books about Tombstone's early years. These two men did not necessarily like each other or remain in touch with each other over the years. Yet each man, independent of the other, stated in their words that Wyatt was a U. S. Deputy Marshal before he came to Tombstone. On October 14, 1881 issues of both the Epitaph and the Nugget newspapers appeared articles stating that U.S. Deputy Marshal Wyatt Earp arrested Frank Stilwell today for robbing the Bisbee Stage, City Marshal Earp arrested Pete Spence. Yet there is the blurb from January 3, 1882 published in the Nugget regarding Wyatt's appointment by telegram after Virgil was ambushed.

There is a great deal of uncertainty regarding the role that Wells Fargo & Company played in the early days of Tombstone, especially regarding the Earp brothers. Three brothers, Wyatt, Morgan and Warren, were employed as messengers, or shotgun guards for the Tombstone stage coaches. There is the $3,000.00 given to Crawley Dake to be used by Wyatt and his posse. But one of the most interesting items is one that appears in a book written by James Hume and John Thacker in 1885. They collaborated on a history of burglaries, stage coach robberies and hold-up's from 1875 to 1885. The two detectives feature various details such as amounts stolen; amounts recovered; drivers and messengers killed and outlaws killed "while resisting arrest." Interestingly, Frank Stilwell is not on this list, but the three men wanted for killing Budd Philpott are. Leonard and Head are correctly listed as dying on June 12, 1881. However, Jim

Crane, who was killed with "Old Man" Clanton on August 13, 1881 in Guadalupe Canyon, is listed as being killed June 13, 1882. This is important in that if the $1,200.00 reward was paid to Wyatt in Colorado on that date, it could have financed a trip to the foothills of the Chiricahua Mountains about one month later when John Ringo was killed. It is also significant in that if the reward was paid to Wyatt in June of 1882, did he and his brothers kill Clanton and the others in Guadalupe Canyon? Since Hume and Thacker's book was not written until three years after they left Tombstone, the Tombstone Office books and the home Office books like the one on the previous page must have been used as date reference. According to the Wells Fargo Archives, the Tombstone Office books were destroyed in the 1906 San Francisco Earthquake. They were the only books destroyed in the 1906 earthquake. Yet in 2000, Robert Chandler, an archivist for Wells Fargo, published the following entry in the Loss and Damage Ledger in True West Magazine:

Courtesy of Robert Chandler, Wells Fargo Archivist

Chandler went on to state that the "@" for Frank Stilwell and "Curly Bill" was an accounting abbreviation of the day, which meant "on account of." This entry could be interpreted to mean that Wells Fargo & Co. paid Wyatt's expenses to kill these two men.

Another unsolved "riddle" deals with the alleged Presidential Pardon for Wyatt and his posse. In the 1920's Wyatt gave an interview to Forrestine Hooker, Henry Hooker's ex-daughter-in-law. Ms. Hooker wrote children's books in Los Angeles at the time, however in this departure she would publish "An Arizona Vendetta" soon after the interview. In this manuscript Wyatt tells a story of being offered the U.S. Marshal's position for Arizona Territory by President McKinley. When he stated he could not return there because of the Frank Stilwell murder warrant, he learned it had been quashed. Wyatt then told that if he and his posse had been extradited; tried and found guilty, President Arthur had said that they would all receive Presidential pardons before they could be sentenced, because in his eyes, they were just Federal Officers doing their duty. This instance, along with the Albuquerque newspaper interview indicates that the President of the United States endorsed Wyatt's actions during the Vendetta Ride. However, as previously mentioned, President Arthur burned his papers the day before he died. Therefore today we can find no provenance for these stories.

The final enigma centers on the death of John Ringo. Wyatt, with the help of his personal secretary John Flood, Jr., wrote an autobiography. It was horrible, and no publishing house would print it. Tom Mix and William S. Hart, the famous silent movie stars, were good friends of Wyatt's and they tried desperately to have the work put out. But even the Saturday Evening Post refused to serialize the work. In this book, as in the Hooker Manuscript, Wyatt states he killed Johnny Ringo. However, he says he did so before he left the Arizona Territory in April 1882. Since Ringo was in Tombstone on July 4, 1882, getting drunk, this story is impossible. Yet, based on Hume and Thacker's "error" regarding Jim Crane's death and the $1,200.00 reward for his death, the window of opportunity opens. If this is what happened and when it happened, July of 1882, according to Crawley Dake, Wyatt was still a U.S. Deputy Marshal. In 1885 Dake was investigated for embezzlement, and in his deposition he stated that he never accepted Wyatt and Virgil's resignations and they were still U.S. Deputy Marshals as far as he was concerned. To date, though, the answers to all these questions remain unanswered, but the search continues. One day we may know.

CHAPTER ELEVEN

Throughout the history of the American West, mining camps and boomtowns saw the "peaks" of prosperity and riches, along with the "valleys" of depleted ores and falling mineral prices. The residents of these communities often times risked their futures and their families' futures on the economically fragile, but occasionally lucrative promise these places offered. It is clear from historic record that more people failed than succeeded in this "winner-take-all" lifestyle that relied on being in the right place at the right time. Like the mines that anchored the monetary stability of the municipality, few of these locales were ever afforded a second chance. However, one of the last major silver-mining boomtowns in the Old West, Tombstone, Arizona Territory, did experience just such a renaissance from 1902 to 1923.

In 1877, Ed Schieffelin discovered silver in the hills approximately 18 miles east of Fort Huachuca. By 1878, he, his brother Albert and Richard Gird had initiated mining operations in these hills, and the village, and soon city that was built around these mines was called Tombstone. As the riches poured out of the hills around the bustling settlement, the population grew almost exponentially. Some sources claim that at one point, Tombstone was the second largest city west of the Mississippi River next to San Francisco, California. It had every commodity and luxury available in the world. Historic architects claim that cement was not used in the West until the last 1890s to early 1900s; yet, the Cosmopolitan Hotel on Allen Street built a cement sidewalk in front of the building in 1880. Next the management planted orange trees out front so their guests could pick fresh fruit while sitting on the veranda. Bourland's Cigar Shop offered its patrons fresh roasted peanuts in 1880 thanks to Edison's new Electric Peanut Roaster. While 110 saloon licenses were allegedly issued, Tombstone also boasted 5 ice cream parlors/saloons. The hotels and restaurants tendered fresh seafood to their customer's every day. Theatrical troupes played at Schieffelin Hall on Fremont Street, which when completed was the largest opera house between El Paso, Texas and San Francisco, California. Just west of town was the Tombstone Driving Park, a racetrack owned by Jack Doling. On the infield of the racetrack, Nellie Cashman built a baseball diamond where the Tombstone baseball team played from 1882 until 1929. The corner of Sixth Street and Fremont Street was the home of the Tombstone Lawn Tennis Association. At the north end of Fifth Street A.J. Mitchell constructed the Tombstone Swimming Baths, a swimming pool. By 1883, there were three water companies, two gas companies and telephone service for the citizens of Tombstone. The populous, at the time, felt their city was going to become as significant as the City by the Bay, and it would have had the price of silver not decreased.

The year 1881 would prove to be the year in history of Tombstone that would root this settlement in the annals of American History. Tombstone became the County Seat for the newly created Cochise County, Arizona Territory. The Earp brothers and "Doc" Holliday engaged in a gun battle with the outlaws known as "Cowboys" in a vacant lot on Fremont Street. Frank and Tom McLaury along with Billy Clanton were killed. The 30-second skirmish received national attention as the repercussions continued for another six months. Lives and reputations were changed, but Tombstone continued to produce silver bullion by the ton. That same year, the mineshafts reached the underground aquifer and the mines flooded. Not to be deterred, two mining operations brought in huge Cornish pumps to continue to chase the veins of ore deeper and deeper into the earth. The engineered strategy caused the Tombstone Hills to again relinquish its precious silver at record rates. Fires ravaged the business district in 1881 and 1882, but the metropolis known as Tombstone rebuilt itself while the ruins still smoldered, integrating more modern conveniences than it had previously.

Eliphalet Butler Gage, more commonly known as E.B. Gage, was a key figure in Tombstone's history from 1879 until 1909. In 1879 at the age of 40, Gage became the Superintendent of the Grand Central Mine, one of the region's largest producers. He was chosen to take the newly formed Arizona Grand Central Mining Company from infancy to profitability, and along with his hand-picked foreman, Charlie Leach, this goal was reached in record time. In six months the Grand Central had produced 2000 tons of ore that had graded out to $100 per ton. To put this into perspective, the $200,000 worth of ore produced would be worth $9,000,000 today. Gage was a "superstar" in Tombstone. His next move was to build a company mill, but his location he chose for the project was either another ingenious savvy move or it was the product of "insider" information. Nine miles downriver from Charleston sat the Contention and Sunset mills. A small community had sprouted from these two worksites, and in July of 1880, it was there that Gage decided to construct the largest ore processing facility in the West. The significance of this decision was that two years later, the town of Contention City would be the closest railroad hub to Tombstone. In order to ensure clear lines of communication within the organization, Gage ordered telephones installed between the Grand Central and Contention Mines in 1881. Subsequently they were installed in the city itself in 1882. Quite an impressive start, but it was only the beginning for E.B. Gage.

Gage became "invested" in the welfare of Tombstone. He was one of the founding members of the Citizen's Safety Committee, along with John Clum, Albert Bilicke, Heyman Solomon, and William Herring to name a few. Although no names were mentioned, it is almost a sure bet that Gage was party to the following article that appeared in the Tombstone Epitaph in April of 1880.

In view of the large element of bad, and in many instances, dangerous characters, in our midst, we learn that the business men and property owners are seriously considering the employment of a secret service officer to keep watch of them. We think the idea an excellent one and we have a party in our mind's eye who is particularly well qualified by previous training to fill the place.

Tombstone Epitaph, April 14, 1880

E. B. Gage's stature in the community made him one of the key "players" in Tombstone during its founding years. His conviction made Gage a staunch supporter of the Earp brothers during their struggles in Tombstone. The actions many have attributed to Gage and others is not documented or reported in the press, yet the names of the prominent men like Gage are mentioned on numerous occasions in later accounts of these turbulent months. It should be pointed out that during the Earp brothers' 28 month residency in Tombstone; the "Cowboys" never committed crimes within the city itself. When Fred White was killed by "curly Bill" Brocius in 1880, it was ruled an accident due to faulty cocking mechanism in Brocius' pistol. The gunfight on Fremont Street between the Earps & Holliday and the Clantons and McLaurys was again essentially an accident. After failing to indict the Earps & Holliday, the "Cowboys" focused their revenge on the Earps, always avoiding the local mining and money magnates. Their superiority lay in sheer numbers. With 75-100 members of the loosely organized gangs, they outnumbered any qualified posse that could be assembled to bring them justice. Through their numbers alone, they were able to intimidate jurors and officers of the court, which allowed them to avoid prosecution. The outlaws knew that should they perpetrate any crime against the corporate and/or mining magnates, these men had the resources to hire qualified posse large enough to exterminate them rather than arrest and prosecute them. In his later years, Wyatt would state that he and his posse were on their way to meet Dan Tipton and O.C. Smith, who were bringing Wyatt $1,000 from Gage, when he killed "Curly Bill" Brocius at Iron Springs in 1882.

The dollar scare of 1885 had an adverse effect on the price of silver, but Tombstone continued to mine ore at a record pace. It was at this time that Gage began to expand his personal holdings. In that same year, E. B. Gage, his brother George, L. W. Blinn, Henry Howe and others invested heavily in the development of the Tempe town site along the Salt River. He also began to explore other mining operations in the territory. The next year, 1886, proved to be the beginning of the end for the Victorian oasis in the southwest Arizona Territory. The pumps of one of Tombstone's primary mines, the Grand Central, burned on May 26th. Almost one year later in 1887, a natural disaster struck that would have economic repercussions over the entire County. A magnitude 7.4 earthquake struck near the small hamlet of Bavispe in Sonora, Mexico, although there was no damage done to the Tombstone mines, the quake completely changed the aquifers in the area. The San Pedro River went underground; the major springs throughout the valleys dried up and fires ravaged the grazing land for livestock. The cattle industry virtually died in southern Cochise County because of this catastrophe. With a price tag of nearly $1,000,000.00 to replace the pumps, owners had to take a hard look at the bottom line. The declining price of silver versus the necessary influx of capital needed resulted in the decision to close these primary producers.

SCENES IN TOMBSTONE.

DECAY OF THE ONCE FAMOUS ARIZONA SILVER CAMP.

I climbed to the summit of the hill on which is situated the reservoir of the Huachuca Water Company, writes a correspondent of the San Francisco Chronicle. Below was the Contention Valley, in the bosom of which nestles the pretty and once prosperous city of Tombstone—name of ill omen. The picture is an exceedingly pretty one to one who loves the mountains and whose heart throbs in unison with the music of the drill and the hammer and the drop of the tireless stamp mill. There is no more picturesque place in Arizona than Tombstone, none more prettily situated, and not one enjoying a more salubrious climate or possessing a more intelligent, enterprising, and generous population.

Its massive blocks and elaborate places of business are reminders of the prosperous days of 1880 to 1883. During that period millions were invested in mining machinery, and within three years more than $5,000,000 were paid out in dividends. Below lay the original discovery of the camp—the Tonghaut Mine. Beyond, to the right, was the Contention, the Grand Central, and other properties that contributed so much to making Tombstone at one time the largest silver producer in the country. I estimated—and it was subsequently confirmed by inquiry at the offices of the mines—that I was looking on hoisting plants and mills that cost fully $5,000,000.

This estimate does not include the long-since-abandoned mills and smelters that line the San Pedro from Benson to Charleston and beyond the Nogales. These latter must have cost several millions more, and stand as reminders of the ignorance of the character of the ores and the means needed for their reduction. To-day but one of them is in operation—the Grand Central mill—but they have had their uses. They furnished the light by means of which their builders and operators were enabled to find the loadstone to attract the precious metals from the ores of Contention Mountain. Having served their purpose they were abandoned, charged to profit and loss, and are now rapidly decaying.

The plants that rested under the eye were no more active than those that fringe the San Pedro. Excepting one little stack on my extreme left, they were all idle. The cages were hanging idle on the cables and rats and lizards inhabited the adits. Of the army of miners, whose monthly pay once aggregated $200,000, less than a hundred are at work to-day. The streets that once swarmed with people are now practically deserted. Blocks of handsome buildings are untenanted. The variety theatre, where serio comics cracked their voices and other people's ears, and where newly made millionaires healed those cracked throats with Jersey champagne at "$5 for pints," only a few years ago, is now vacant, dark, and dreary, the boxes, that hang like birdcages from the sides, still carrying a suggestion of wicked women, wasted lives, empty purses, and headaches. Three banks have given way to one, and over the whole hovers the evil spirit of desolation.

The transition came as in a night. With the dying out of the flames of the Grand Central in 1885 came the gloom that has since hung over the place. The great strike two years before was an injury to the camp, and it had scarcely recovered from that when the other disaster came. Five years of idleness; five years of contraction of values, of detraction outside, of waiting. And yet there are here brave spirits who have never wavered, never despaired. Through it all they have stood by Tombstone, and express a determination to do so to the end. The attachment men form for a mining camp is stronger than that for any other locality. In the end these loyal Tombstoners will get their reward.

More disastrous than strike, fire, or water was the act demonetizing silver. That law paralyzed the entire camp. The Grand Central Company did not feel warranted to replace a pumping plant that cost between $350,000 and $400,000. Soon others ceased pumping, and the water gradually rose, and no one could work below the water level.

While work was prosecuted below that level no change was found either in the value or the characteristics of the ores. There was no reason to believe that with silver at a fair price the large dividends should not be continued indefinitely. Those riches are still in these mines, under the water. They cannot be reached unless the water is lifted, and that means the expenditure of a sum approximating $1,000,000. No one company feels like going to this expense, since its pumping would help all its neighbors; indeed, every mine in the camp. Efforts have been made to consolidate the great interests of the camp and jointly erect a pumping plant, but without success thus far. All miners agree that the body of water encountered in this camp is enormous; indeed, that it is quite phenomenal; but with silver permanently at from $1.15 to $1.20 this difficulty would be soon overcome and Tombstone would once more be itself.

By 1889, the mines had closed, and the population had dwindled. Some of the inhabitants moved to the copper mining community, Bisbee a mere 23 miles south of Tombstone, while others moved further west top the various mining districts around Patagonia. At this point, it looked as though Tombstone was destined to become another uninhabited footnote in the mining history of the Old West. The pessimists that reveled in Tombstone's fall from grace pronounced the town doomed in 1894 when Gage left for the Congress Mine in Yavapai County. Several key engineers and miners accompanied Gage in this new venture.

Remnants of the early mining works circa 1902

The Business District at 4th and Allen Streets circa 1902
Harper's Weekly
May 17, 1902

One characteristic of the Tombstone Hills that kept hopes alive was the fact that these hills were rich in other minerals in addition to silver. For three decades, Gage would play a pivotal role in Tombstone's development from its tumultuous early years to becoming the catalyst for the town's resurgence into the Twentieth Century. It would be this diversity along with the courage and vision of E.B. Gage that would resurrect the mining industry and the City of Tombstone.

Eliphalet Butler Gage
Author's Collection

CHAPTER TWELVE

The stereotypical image of a scruffy old man with a pick and a mule was a far cry from the reality of mining precious metals. Mining in the 1880's was a very labor intensive process. It involved excavation and shaft construction; two-man drilling teams to create blasting holes; blasters breaking loose the ore with black powder or dynamite; mockers collecting the ore fragments from the blast; constructing hoists or whims to retrieve the ore out of the shaft; freighting the ore to the mills along the San Pedro River to be converted in to bullion and finally shipping the bullion to a destination. Although a "modern-day practice," this method of mining was inherently dangerous. The deeper the shafts went, the greater the danger. Fatal accidents were common but an accepted risk the laborers took. Many men and many steps were necessary to transform the tons of "rocks" into shiny bricks of silver. The silver ore in and around Tombstone was of such a high grade, that even after paying top wages to the men performing these tasks, the mining magnates still realized substantial profits and wealth.

Unlike the placer mining associated with the California gold rush, which relied on flumes and water to locate the mineral, the Tombstone district relied on hard-rock mining. There were two primary methods, shafts & drifts and stoping. With shafts & drifts, a vertical shaft was excavated, and then horizontal shafts extended from the main shaft, which led to "rooms" that were dug out to mine the ore veins at different levels.

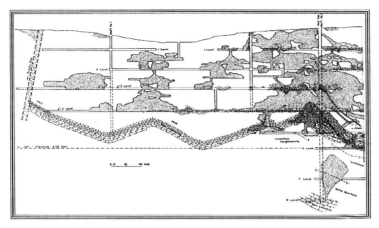

Shafts and Drifts
Author's Collection

The other hard-rock mining method of the day was stoping. In stoping the shaft would follow the vein of ore as it sank lower into the earth, and the miners would "stair-step" down into the earth to ensure all of the ore had been extracted. Areas similar to drifts would be excavated at each level to maximize the mining operation.

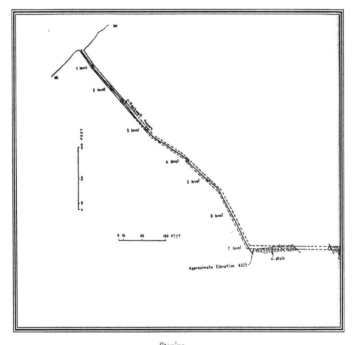

Stoping
Author's Collection

The most famous, or infamous, example of stoping was the Good Enough Mine located near the intersection of 5th and Toughnut Streets in Tombstone. It was called "The Million Dollar Stope," because almost $1,000,000 worth of silver was mined from this claim. Unfortunately, in their exuberance to mine all of the ore they could find, the management of the Good Enough Mine directed their miners to dig too close to the streets. In 1894, as an ice wagon passed through the intersection, the street collapsed. Horse and driver were saved, but the wagon and its cargo were lost. This incident was repeated in 1994. Current structural upgrades have been installed to prevent any similar accidents in the future. The Good Enough Mine, though, was not the only shaft or stope to venture underneath the city streets, as can be seen in the following illustration, but it is the only one you can tour today.

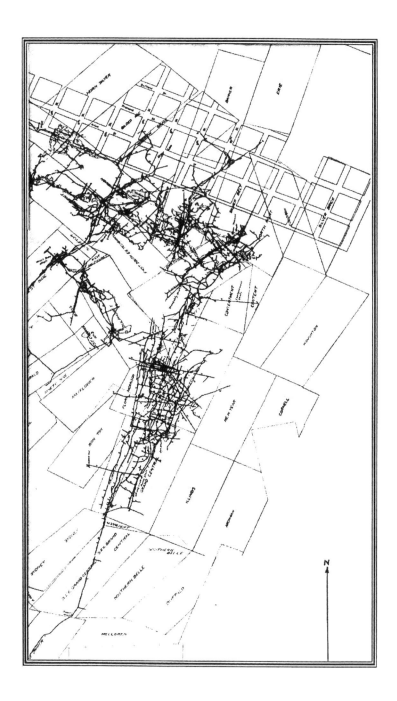

Map of Mineshafts
Author's Collection

In contrast to its many predecessors, Tombstone's precious mineral deposits were not depleted during its initial boom. Mother Nature and the volatility of the economy had caused the city to dwindle in the late 1880's and early 1900's. Independent lessees continued mining operations on a few of the claims, but the primary industry became Cochise County government in Tombstone. As stated before, E.B. Gage's departure for Yavapai County in 1894 drained the ranks of the best mining men in Tombstone. In 1895, rancher John Pearce discovered a gold bonanza on his ranch in the eastern foothills of the Dragoon Mountains, not far from the former silver Mecca. This find was between five and eight feet wide and extended for five and six hundred yards in length. The news of this discovery caused the hasty exodus of many of the remaining miners and speculators in Tombstone. In 1897, Tombstone's founding Father, Ed Schieffelin died of an apparent heart attack near Canyonville, Oregon at the age of 49. At his request, his body was interred on one of his early campsites a few miles west of the city, and a 25 foot tall monument was completed in November of 1897 to mark the grave. The city floundered for the next five years. Banks and merchants came and went, however, there always seemed to be a resident willing to step up and fill the void in the business community. When the 1899 national statistics were published in Tombstone's local newspaper, **The Prospector**, on January 2, 1900, the Arizona Territory ranked seventh in the production of gold and fifth in the output of silver.

METAL PRODUCTION

How Arizona Compares With Other States.

The preliminary estimate of the production of gold and silver in the United States during the year 1899 made by the U.S. Statiscan shows the total gold production to be $71,694,-170, an increase over last year of $6,236,670; silver, $74,244,696, an increase of $4,040,211. The gold and silver production by states in 1899 is given as follows:

States.	Gold.	States.	Silver.
Nevada	$ 2,442,000	Nevada	$ 1,254,800
Washington	506,202	Washington	452,525
Oregon	1,550,387	Oregon	193,940
Alaska	4,603,819	Alaska	258,585
California	14,952,392	California	1,396,963
Idaho	2,480,620	Idaho	5,171,717
Montana	4,919,897	Montana	20,040,403
Utah	3,369,509	Utah	9,696,669
Apalachian States	337,334	Apalachian States	9,057
Colorado	26,000,000	Colorado	31,208,037
South Dakota	6,120,000	South Dakota	550,700
Arizona	2,500,000	Arizona	3,000,000
New Mexico	600,000	New Mexico	600,000
Wyoming	6,000	Texas	600,000
Totals	$71,694,170	Total	$70,604,770

The Tombstone Prospector, January 2, 1900

The level of economic ruin can be seen in the following notice of sale for delinquent taxes by the Sheriff office:

Sheriff's Sale of Mining Claims.

By virtue of an execution issued out of the District Court of the First Judicial District of the Territory of Arizona in and for Cochise County, dated the 5th day of December 1899, upon a judgment duly rendered in said court in the case entitled Martyn Bonnell vs. Grand Central Mining Company, No. 2099, wherein the said Martyn Bonnell as plaintiff, recovered a judgment against the said Grand Central Mining Company, as defendant, for the sum of two hundred and four thousand nine hundred and fifty five 97-100 ($204,955.97) dollars, costs included, on the 4th day of December 1899, by which I am commanded to make the said sum of money with interest at seven per cent. er annum from December 4th 1899, out of the personal property of the said Grand Central Mining Company, or if sufficient thereof cannot be found, then out of the real property belonging to said defendant on the said 4th day of December 1899, or any time since.

And whereas, sufficient personal property of the said defendant cannot be found in my county out of which to make said sum of money, I have levied on and siezed all of the right title and interest which the said defendant had on the said 4th day of December 1899, or at any time since, in and to the several mining claims and patented mines situated in the Tombstone Mining District, Cochise County, Arizona Territory the location notices of which and the patents of said Cochise County in the Books of Records of Mines and Deeds of Mines respectively as follows, to-wit:

The U. S. Patented Mine Alkey, No. 14930 Recorded in Book 12 Deeds of Mines, at page 261

The U. S. Patented Mine Hidden Treasure, No. 25510. Recorded in Book 11 Deeds of Mines, at page 557.

The U. S. Patented Mine Last Chance No. 2, 21679, Recorded in Book 11, at page 553. Deeds of Mines.

The U. S. Patented Mine Silver Thread, No. 16984, recorded in Book 11, Deeds of Mines, at Page 564.

The U. S. Patented Mine Chance, No. 24443, recorded in Book 11, Deeds of Mines, at page 550.

The U. S. Patented Mine Standard No. 24325, recorded in Book 11, Deeds of Mines, at page 547.

The U. S. Patented Mine Moonlight, No. 14658, recorded in Book 11, Deeds of Mines, at page 543.

The U. S. Patented Mine Naumkeag, No. 5403, recorded in Book V, Deeds of Mines, at page 17.

The U. S. Patented Mine Grand Central No. 5352, recorded in Book 5, Deeds of Mines, at page 24.

The U. S. Patented Mine Extacy No. 7420, recorded in Book 8, Deeds of Mines, at page 87.

The U. S. Patented Mine Shorty, No. 7419, recorded in Book 8, Deeds of Mines, at page 93.

The U. S. Patented Mine Maine No. 9933, recorded in Book 8, Deeds of Mines, at page 510.

The U. S. Patented Mine Mexican, No. 12306, recorded in Book 9, Deeds of Mines, at page 541.

The U. S. Patented Mine Revenue No. 12797, recorded in Book 11, Deeds of Mines at page 24.

The U. S. Patented Mine Contact, No. 12305, recorded in Book 9, Deeds of Mines, at page 536.

The U. S. Patented Mine Tripple Ex. No. 9931, recorded in Book 8, Deeds of Mines, at page 536.

The U. S. Patented Mine Emerald No. 9998, recorded in Book 8, Deeds of Mines, at page 600.

The U. S. Patented Mine Grand Dipper No. 9997, recorded in Book 8, Deeds of Mines, at page 606.

The U. S. Patented Mine Brother Jonathan No. 9932, recorded in Book 8, Deeds of Mines, at page 530.

The Ouoopah Mining Claim, location notice of which is recorded in Book 3, Transcribed Records of Pima County, Record of Mines, at page 547.

The Central Mining Claim, location notice of which is recorded in Book 6, Transcribed Records of Pima County, Records of Mines, at page 66n.

The Lowell Mining Claim, location notice of which is recorded in Book 7, Records of Mines, at page 337, Cochise County Records.

The North Point Mining Claim, location notice of which is recorded in Book 1, Transcribed Records of Pima County, Record of Mines, at page 359.

The Boss Mining Claim, location notice of which is recorded in Book 2, Transcribed Records of Pima County, Record of Mines, at page 131.

Those two certain dwelling houses, three small houses, one stable building, assay office, shop, boiler house, and one hoisting engine partly erected, situated upon the Grand Central Mine.

One dwelling house, one shaft house and hoisting engine, situated on the Maine Mine.

One shaft house, one hoisting engine and boilers and three small houses, situated upon the Emerald Mine.

One shaft house with engine and boiler, situated upon the Silver Thread Mine.

One engine and boiler, one shop and one ore house, situated upon the Chance Mine.

One boiler house with boiler, situated upon the Boss Mining Claim.

One thirty-stamp quartz mill, situated on the San Pedro River, near the town of Fairbanks, known as the Grand Central Mill.

All of the tools, lathes, and old machinery now on the dumps and upon the property hereinbefore described.

Public notice is hereby given that on Wednesday the 10th day of January, A. D. 1900, at ten o'clock in the forenoon of that day, in front of the Court House door of said Cochise County, at the City of Tombstone, Arizona, I will sell at public auction to the highest and best bidder for cash, currency of the United States, all of the above described property, or so much thereof as may be necessary to satisfy said judgment and costs and accruing costs.

Dated at Tombstone, Arizona, December 19, 1899.

SCOTT WHITE,
Sheriff.
By GEO. BRAVIN,
Deputy Sheriff.

n-19

The Tombstone Prospector, January 8, 1900

There are several claims of note listed here, The Last Chance, The Grand Central and The Emerald. All were big producers during Tombstone's early years, yet they were for sale to settle claims against the original owners, The Grand Central Mining Company. E.B. Gage's influence was still felt in Tombstone, as his visits generated a sense of excitement and hope for a rejuvenation of mining in the hill surrounding the town. William (Billy) Hattich, owner and editor of *The Prospector*, began to publish Gage's visits to Tombstone from Yavapai County. Hattich was the quintessential optimist. As with most residents of Tombstone, Hattich would report their travels as well; however, Gage's movements always maintained a mysterious tone, due in part to Hattich's enthusiasm. Hattich had arrived in Tombstone with his father in 1880. Growing up and going to school during Tombstone's early years, Billy Hattich had seen first-hand the astronomical growth and prosperity silver mining had brought to the area. Upon his arrival, he could have tasted fresh oysters at the Rockaway Oyster House or pate in the Fountain underneath The Grand Hotel. In short, Billy Hattich would have seen Tombstone in its finest moments, and he had returned from California in time to see it in one of its worst. Throughout the stark contrast, Hattich maintained a positive, forward-thinking approach to both the news and Tombstone's future. Whenever possible he could and would spin any mining report into a positive outlook for the return of the industry to Tombstone.

The spring of 1900 saw The Prospector reporting all of Gage's visits to and from Tombstone, but there was never any conclusive report of a return of mining to Tombstone. Finally in June of 1900, the report Hattich and the town had been waiting for hit the news wires, and it was promptly displayed at the top of the local page on June 2, 1900. E.B. Gage and his partner Frank Murphy had sold their Congress mine for $3,000,000 to Warner Miller, a New York millionaire.

BIG MINING SALE

The Congress Mine Sells For Three Million Dollars

The Gazette says: After years of working, the Congress mine has been sold, and that at a figure that is astounding. Warner Miller, the New York millionaire, is at the head of the syndicate that has purchased the Congress mine and the price paid is $3,000,000. The money was paid through the Chase National bank in New York and E B Gage and Frank Murphy get the bulk of this enormous sum. Senator Miller made four different examinations of the property before purchasing, but during his last visit in March he made up his mind to buy the property, and the Congress mine is now in his hands and his company is operating it.

The mine has been worked for the past six years with a profit of from $30,000 to $75,000 per month and is without doubt one of Arizona's greatest mines.

The Tombstone Prospector, June 2, 1900

To put this in perspective and using the Gross Domestic Product Index, today the sale would equal approximately $75,000,000, and monthly profits would equal $150,000 to $1,875,000 per month. Now Gage had the capital to begin an even grander venture back in Tombstone, and Hattich lost no time in announcing the fact to the local population.

> **REOPEN GRAND CENTRAL**
>
> ### Sale of the Congress May Mean Much for Tombstone
>
> With the sale of the Congress mine for $3,000,000, E B Gage, one of the principal owners, secures a fortune for his interest. Mr Gage is largely interested in the Grand Central Co, of Tombstone and it is not unlikely that the well known mining man will now turn his attention to the property in which he was instrumental in making one of the famous mines of Arizona and ranking among the best producing properties in the west. The Grand Central has yet a brilliant future before it and with the resumption of work can be listed among the big paying mines of the west. It has been accredited to Mr Gage that at such time when he could again give entire time and attention to the undertaking, he would endeavor to reopen the big property here, whose merits and value he has never doubted. With the disposal of his interests at Congress it is now reasonable to believe and fondly hoped that he will turn his attention this way.

The Tombstone Prospector, June 4, 1900

This was "just what the doctor ordered" in Hattich's eyes. Throughout the summer of 1900 he documented Gage's every move in and around Tombstone and continuously prophesied the end to Tombstone's economic devastation.

Although Gage's share of the sale of the Congress Mine was substantial, he knew two things from his earlier days in Tombstone. First, the huge Cornish pumps installed at the Contention and Grand Central mines had lowered the water levels in <u>all</u> of the mines and, in order to make his new vision for mining in the Tombstone District work, he would need more capital. This sent Gage and his inner circle to New York to sell the investment world on his plans for resurrecting the Tombstone Mining District under one company, one management group and, foremost, under the watchful eye of E.B. Gage. At the time Wall Street was beginning to buzz, like Hattich, about the potential wealth that lay submerged in Tombstone. The site's track record was well documented, and with the resurgence in the price of silver, more doors were opening in the financial arena. E.B. Gage and Frank Murphy, his partner in the Congress Mine, leverage their $3,000,000 into $18,000,000 and the shopping spree was on. The second quarter of 1900 would see Gage and his new company, Tombstone Consolidated Mines Company, acquire some 90% of the working claims in the Tombstone Hills. Approximately five square miles of mining claims was now under the umbrella of Tombstone Consolidated. These transactions expended about $2,000,000 leaving the company enough capital to rehabilitate, restore and replace, as needed, the existing mining works abandoned over a decade ago.

Tombstone Consolidated Mines Company stock certificate
Author's Collection

Later the company would sell contract bonds for capital.

**Tombstone Consolidated Mines Company
contract bond certificate
Author's Collection**

As work progressed in the hills above Tombstone, Gage unveiled his plan for Tombstone Consolidated Mines Company. He knew that only having two large Cornish pumps to lower the water level in all of the miens had been the fatal flaw in the 1880's. Therefore, he proposed to install a system of pumps at various levels to ensure that Tombstone Consolidated Mines Company would not suffer the same setback that has befallen the Arizona Grand Central Mining Company. This would prevent a catastrophe should one of the pumps become disabled. There would be enough pumping power in reserve to continue mining operations until the damaged unit could be repaired or replaced. With control of over 90% of the mining property in the Tombstone Mining District, Gage and Tombstone Consolidated Mines Company were not going to risk losing their next fortune on any mechanical failure. Gage and William F. Staunton had devised a plan to create a four-compartment shaft, which would allow two to be used for hoisting ore out of the shafts and two for the pumping operation.

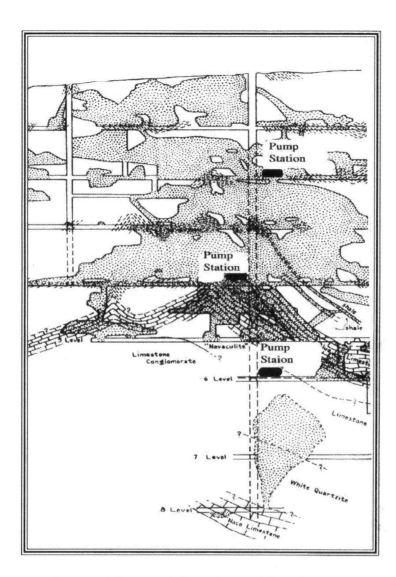

Conceptual Drawing of Gage's Proposed Pumping Stations
Author's Collection

Staunton had joined the Tombstone mining community in 1883, and was brought in by Gage to oversee the Congress Mine when his good friend and college, Charlie Leach, accidentally killed himself when he failed to properly put out a gas lamp one night before bed. With capital, concept and construction all in place, the Tombstone Mining District and the city were on the verge of the second mining boom.

CHAPTER THIRTEEN

One of the great oddities and more fascinating facts of Tombstone's first mining boom was that this financial metropolis sprang out of the Southwestern Arizona desert without a railroad. The ore was hauled by wagon to the San Pedro River, and the processed bullion was freighted out through Wells Fargo & Company by stagecoach. By 1901 the closest railroad terminal was located in Fairbank, approximately nine miles north of Tombstone. Because all of the abandoned equipment still in place was decades old and extremely obsolete, all new boilers, hoists, pumps, wenches, etc. had to be freighted in again. There was an additional problem facing Tombstone Consolidated Mines Company, the size of the equipment required to achieve their goals was going to be much larger than had ever been used in the district before. Gage and Murphy would face the same dilemma of freighting in their new boilers, mining machinery and pumps with draft horses or mules and wagons. While men worked to rebuild the mines as well as construct a new four-compartment shaft, the brain trust of Tombstone Consolidated Mines Company began working on these logical issues.

Great progress was made throughout 1901 in the mines. Shafts were completed and new drifts were cut connecting the Grand Central and Contention mines. In November, the shaft reached the water at the 569 foot level. The new mining machinery began arriving in Fairbank by January of 1902, and it was time to reveal Gage's and Murphy's solution. Special wagons had been built in Fairbank with six-foot diameter rear wheels and four-foot diameter front wheels to haul the massive boilers for the pumps. Eleven months after their arrival the first pump was loaded onto its special wagon, but the 34 horses labored to move the monstrous boiler 500 yards. Ten days later and using teams of up to 52 horses, the first boiler was delivered to the mine. The second boiler soon followed. Like the wagons, the pumps were custom made to Tombstone

Consolidated Mines Company specifications. Their normal capacity was 1,500 gallons per minute, but they had the capability to remove up to 2,000 gallons per minute. With maximum steam, these pumps could expel 2,500,000 gallons in a 24 hour period. All the while, a new 79-foot tall steel head frame was built and installed in cement above the mineshaft. Its width at the base was 30 feet across. Tombstone Consolidated Mines Company has some 100 men scurrying about the Tombstone Hills installing the pumps and other machinery as they arrived. It was reminiscent of the early mining days two decades earlier. As 1902 came to a close, all of the pumping apparatus has been tested, and the shaft had reached below the water level. The era of Tombstone Consolidated Mines Company was about to move Tombstone into the Twentieth Century the same way it had begun, on the grandest of scales.

Just as in Tombstone's inception, soon the sounds of construction were not limited to the mines on the hills. They were heard echoing throughout the business district as well. Merchants and businessmen got ready for the new mining boom by renovating many of the existing structures, while other entrepreneurs had plans drawn for their new venture. Unlike Tombstone's initial boom, this time the business district remained a single-story skyline. The two and three-story structures that had risen from the streets would not be resurrected. However, to keep up with the times, many businessmen merely had new fronts built onto the existing structure to visually present a modern façade. Preparations were underway to meet the demands of the new wave of residents with new stores, hotels, restaurants and of course saloons. Harper's Weekly ran an article touting Tombstone's new resurgence and revival:

"TOMBSTONE IS ALREADY LOOKING UP. PEOPLE WHO HAVE HUNG ON DURING THE DULL DAYS NOW ENJOY RENEWED HOPE. OLD BUILDINGS ARE BEING CLEANED OUT, AND PEOPLE ARE MOVING IN. THE DAILY STAGE BRINGS TO TOMBSTONE MINING EXPERTS, AND MINER, AND THEIR FACES ARE EAGERLY SCANNED BY THE OLD INHABITANTS, FOR IT HAS BEEN A LONG TIME SINCE THE PLEASURE OF NEW ACQUAINTANCES HAS BEEN GIVEN THEM.

"THE TOMBSTONE OF THE FUTURE WILL NEVER BE THE TOMBSTONE OF THE PAST. IT WILL LOSE THE PICTURESQUES FEATURES COMMON TO ALL BIG WESTERN MINING-CAMPS IN THE EARLY DAYS, BUT THE PROPECTS ARE GOOD FOR A LARGE AND PROSPEROUS CAMP, PLENTY OF MINES OPERATED REGULARLY, BIG PAY-ROLLS, SMELTERS WITH THEIR MANY SIDE INDUSTRIES, AND NEW RAILROADS. INDEED THE SURVEYORS ARE NOW IN FIELD MARKING THE LINE FOR AN EXTENTION OF THE ROCK ISLAND RAILROAD, WHICH WILL MAKE TOMBSTONE ONE OF ITS PRINCIPAL STATIONS. THIS INDEED WILL NOT BE THE TOMBSTONE OF THE EARLY EIGHTIES, BUT ITS NEW PROSPERITY WILL BE BUILT UPON A MORE SOLID FOUNDATION AND IT WILL BECOME GREATER THAN EVER."

Harper's Weekly, May 17, 1902

Although the second coming of silver in Tombstone did not entice men like John Clum, Jack Doling, Lou Rickabaugh or other early prominent entrepreneurs to return, a new echelon of pioneer businessmen and families rose to prominence as Tombstone returned to life. The Cosmopolitan Hotel and the Occidental Hotel were long gone, but the Macia family converted an adobe lodging house from the 1880's into the Arcade Hotel. Plating was added to the exterior as was this extremely ornate cornice work around the top.

Arcade Hotel
Author's Collection

F.N. Wolcott, who settled in Tombstone in 1881, owned one of the town's oldest general merchant stores. Wolcott's was located on the corner of 4th and Allen Street, which had been the site of Tombstone's leading mercantile dating back to 1879 when John "Pie" Allen opened the first general store in the camp.

F.N. Wolcott's Store
Author's Collection

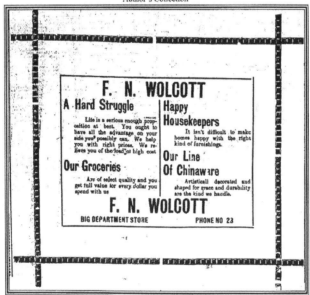

The Tombstone Prospector, 1903
Courtesy of the Arizona State Library & Archives

W. A. "Billy" King had come to Cochise County in 1883. In the late 1890s, king purchased the property that had been Hafford's Saloon on the northeast corner of 4th and Allen Streets. It was here that the Earp brothers and "Doc" Holliday met on October 26, 1881 before their fateful walk down Fremont Street.

"Billy" King's O.K. Saloon
Author's Collection

The Tombstone Prospector, 1903
Courtesy of the Arizona State Library & Archives

Paul B. Warnerkos had come to Tombstone in 1878 and secured a position as a clerk for P. W. Smith at the store Smith had purchased from "Pie" Allen. In the late 1880's, Warnerkos opened the Ranchers and Miners Supply Store and in later years invested heavily in real estate. Over the years, he owned, among other holdings, Schieffelin Hall. At the time of Tombstone's second mining boom, Mr. Warnerkos was its longest continuous resident.

Paul B. Warnekos   The Tombstone Prospector, 1903

Frank Yaple and Frank Moreno formed a partnership in 1902 that blended the new and the old. Yaple had arrived in Tombstone in 1880 and opened a sewing machine store. Although his initial business was destroyed by fire, Yaple relocated and continued to serve as a leader in Tombstone's business community. Frank Moreno, 25 years old at the time of the partnership, provided both youth and experience to the enterprise.

Yaple & Moreno's Store
Author's Collection

On page 4 is a picture of Allen Street before the rehabilitation of the business district began. In the front right one can see the remnants of the original first floor below the Occidental Hotel. A major merchant from Bisbee acquired the property and it became the home to the Machomich Mercantile. As can be seen from its photograph, this building reflected the architectural influences of the early Twentieth Century, not those of the Victorian 1880's.

The Machomich Building
Author's Collection

The stalwart of all the businessmen was a man who played a continuous role in Tombstone and in the Arizona Territory throughout its early years, L.W. Blinn. Blinn, a lumber magnate, opened his outlet in Tombstone in 1880. He played significant roles in business, land development, politics and recreation.

L.W. Blinn Lumber Company
Author's Collection

The stage was set. Tombstone Consolidated Mines Company had implemented a new, large-scale mining operation, while new and old businessmen had prepared their merchandise assortments to meet the needs of the rapidly rising population. The only thing missing from this dynamic mix was a railroad, but Gage & company already had plans in the works to remedy this deficit as well.

CHAPTER FOURTEEN

From the beginning, Gage had intended that all of the new mining and pumping equipment for Tombstone Consolidated Mines Company would arrive in Tombstone by rail. However, no railroad had ever reached Tombstone during or after the first mining boom. Phelps-Dodge, the copper mining conglomerate in Bisbee had bypassed Tombstone in 1888 when it built the El Paso-Southwestern Railroad between Bisbee and Fairbank. In 1897, there had been random speculation that the growing interest in the Tombstone Mining District might result in a railroad, but again, nothing came to fruition. Tombstone Consolidated Mines Company had hoped to persuade Phelps-Dodge to build a Tombstone spur, but the copper magnate seemed unwilling to assist. Gage, however, had an "ace" up his sleeve, his partner Frank Murphy. Murphy had very strong ties to the Southern Pacific Railroad. Using this relationship, Tombstone Consolidated Mines Company, for lack of a better word, "extorted" a railroad spur to Tombstone from Phelps-Dodge.

The Tombstone Prospector, January 10, 1903

Survey crews began their trek from Fairbank in the summer of 1901. These crews survey several potential courses for the railroad extension. The route chosen made its way up Walnut Gulch from Fairbank, around Comstock Hill on the western outskirts of Tombstone, then mirroring the city limits, it wound around to the southern side of the city a station site near 4th and Toughnut Streets. From the station, the tracks veered onto Allen Street past 10th Street, and then Tombstone Consolidated Mines Company constructed an extension up into the mining district to the complex surrounding the pump shaft atop Contention Hill. Crews began blasting, grading and leveling on July 29, 1902. Although the work went quickly and smoothly, the actual laying of the track did not begin until March of 1903. Like the creation of the railroad bed, the track laying took little time. Regular passenger train service officially began April 5, 1903, and on April 12, 1903 the onset of rail service in Tombstone was celebrated with dignitaries, barbecue and, of course, speeches. Tombstone now had a cost-effective method to connect to the rest of the nation and the world.

The Tombstone Prospector, April 13, 1903

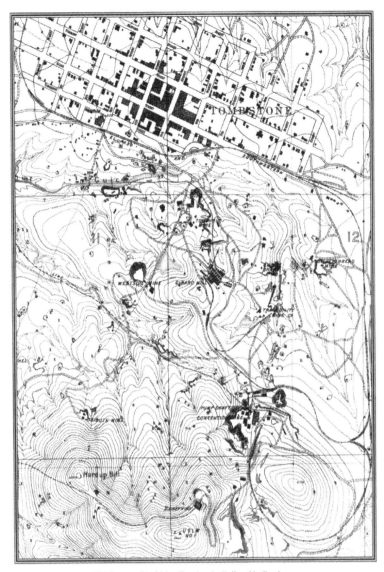

1908 Topographical Map Showing the Railroad in Tombstone
Author's Collection

All the while, the mining operations continued to proceed. As of June, 1903, the water level in all of the mines had been successfully lowered, despite the fact that the pumps were not yet able to operate at peak capacity yet. By the middle of June the pumps were draining 2,225,000 gallons of water per day. To date, Tombstone Consolidated Mines Company had avoided the two keys to disaster in their new venture, mechanical failure and human error. The latter would occur in a matter of weeks. A lone pump-man lowered the valve controlling the steam to the pumps, and went to the surface for an hour. Upon his return he found the station flooded and all of the pumps shut down. Panic set in. Soon the water had risen leaving the valve sixty feet below the water's surface. The only way to reach the valve and open it again would be with divers, and Tombstone Consolidated Mines Company immediately brought in two of them from San Francisco. In less time than it took to write with paragraph, the pumping machinery was back in operation, and soon the water level returned to normal.

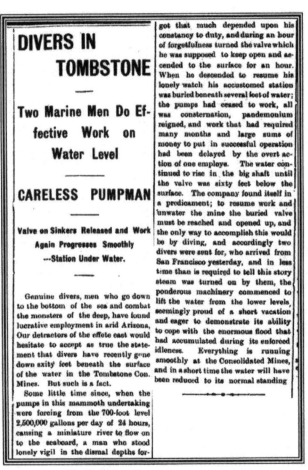

The Tombstone Prospector, June 19, 1903

The hierarchy of Tombstone Consolidated Mines Company could neither afford nor want a repeat of this episode. To ensure against this and/or any other malfunction, another large boiler was brought in November, resulting in five carloads of ore being shipped to the smelters in El Paso that month, and by December four carloads a day were steaming out of Tombstone for processing. These include not only the sulphide ore, but significant levels of gold as well. The City of Tombstone, its mines and its railroad, were all booming again. As the reporter from Harper's Weekly had predicted, it was not the Tombstone of old.

The year 1903 had breathed life back into Tombstone. For the remainder of the year, Billy Hattich reported on events like the expansion of the Cochise County Courthouse. On January 6th the first automobile was seen in Tombstone, and some seven months later E.B. Gage purchased one. The emergence of six banks in Cochise County was noted; stating that in the prior year there had been none. He also documented the rising silver prices and the creation of new, albeit smaller, mining corporations. There were many accounts of the success of Tombstone's baseball team. The Tombstone School District reported an enrollment of 250 students in the Fall of 1903. Tombstone was a thriving 20th Century community filled with hope, optimism and vision.

> A new automobile arrived today for President E. B. Gage of the Con. Mines Co. It is a Cadillac make and is being set up at King's blacksmith's shop. Another larger auto is expected to arrive this week also.

The Tombstone Prospector, August 6, 1903
Courtesy of the Arizona State Library & Archives

> **Price of Silver Climbing Up**
>
> A New York dispatch dated August 25th, says bar silver reached the highest price today for many years, it being quoted at 56¼. The advance in the price of the white metal is largely due to the demand from England which has been constantly increasing for several months.
>
> Six months ago the price ranged from 51 to 45, but since there has been an increased demand from Europe and the price has been gradually moving upward.

The Tombstone Prospector, August 27, 1903
Courtesy of the Arizona State Library & Archives

The year ended with a very genuine and grateful editorial from Hattich. The last newspaper of the year also included a "tribute" article to the men of Tombstone Consolidated Mines Company in acknowledgement of their accomplishments.

THE OLD AND THE NEW

A Fond Farewell and a Most Generous Greeting

AUSPICIOUS ARRIVAL.

The Old Year Glides by Conscious of Having Done Nobly---The New Year Comes Laden With Joy

The gentle tread of Father Time causes one to hearken; the old year is about to make its exit as the new one comes apace. The Christian world hails with delight the new calendar year of 1904, not oblivious of the fact, however, that 1903 has been prolific with good to mankind, and as each succeeding year rivals its predecessor the universe, as if by one voice, acclaims a hearty greeting for the New Year, laden with joys and expectancies, the fulfillment of which fills the heart of man with gratitude, and though his allotted time may nearly have expired and the light over yonder signals him hither, he gives generous welcome and unreserved cheer to the New Year that cuts short his span of life. Grateful, unselfish man who can cheerfully welcome the approach of that which lessens his days of existence. Tomorrow the New Year breaks in up us; all hail the New Year!

While the world in general is joyous with hope and anticipation, we should not be forgetful of the beneficence showered upon us during 1903; the sciences have been enriched far greater than the students hoped for; the arts have shared correspondingly; improvements in mechanism have astounded the universe and onward and upward marked the endeavors of the multitude.

The southwest has been generally blessed, the Pacific coast unsparingly favored, while Arizona in particular has prospered. Cochise county has made great strides; her herds have flourished and multiplied, while many new mines have been opened up and made to yield bounteously. In Tombstone the progress of one year is discernable; Twelve months ago we were without railway connection, we had no banking institution, but one system of water works, and the great pumps that were to unwater the mines were not yet in place, but today reveals all these deficiencies met and overcome; many improvements have resulted and the present augurs brightly for the future. Let us feel grateful for the many blessings of 1903; let the community stand as one man in the line of progress, and our efforts of 1904 will be rewarded by still greater achievements. To the year 1904 we respectfully salute!

DRAINING THE DISTRICT

A Remarkable Showing by the Big Pumps on the Hill

SECOND PUMP NOW IN

The Unwatering of the Tombstone Levels No Longer a Problem---Will Go Down 1,000 Feet

The big pumps on the 700-foot level of the Tombstone Con. Co. shaft were in operation this week and work as smooth and satisfactory as could possibly be expected of the mammoth machinery. These pumps are a duplicate of the large station pumps on the 600 level and has been installed as a relief for its mate, the lower pumps being 100 feet below the water level. The daily capacity of the station pumps are 2,500,000 gallons each, the lower pump draining the incoming flow and sending the same to the reservoir on the level, 100 feet above; from here, the first duplex pumps continue the lift to the surface. Should an accident happen to one, the other is capable of handling the water to the surface independently and sinking pumps held in constant reserve make the probability of any trouble with the machinery or unexpected inflow of water an obstacle to be readily overcome.

Since the working of the pumps on the 700-foot level, drifting has been started and the work on this level will be crowded ahead, considerable headway having already been made. But little trouble is being experienced with the water, and as a conclusive indication that the inflow of water on the 700 is diminishing, the pumping record shows a gradual decrease. A comparison of the record of the past 20 days shows over 250,000 gallons less daily during that period, the record for yesterday being considerably below the 2,000,000-gallon mark. These facts are indeed most encouraging and show that the mine drainage problem in the Tombstone district is being solved beyond a question and the unerring judgment of President E. B. Gage and General Manager W. F. Staunton in this successful demonstration is evidenced.

The company is arranging to begin the sinking of the big shaft to 1000 feet. The preparatory work of continuing the sinking of the shaft has already been ordered, and with the start of the new year will be under way. The new year opens auspiciously for the Tombstone Consolidated Company and will be one of great promise for its fortunate owners.

CHAPTER FIFTEEN

The City of Tombstone, The Tombstone Mining District and Cochise County rode the current prosperity mining had brought with the new century. Tombstone Consolidated Mines Company sustained its cutting-edge approach by restoring and opening many of the old mines, while pushing the Boom Shaft closer and closer to the 1000 foot depth. The ingenious system maintained its record-setting performances by surpassing each milestone. Over the next four years the pumps' output would surpass the 3,000,000 gallons-per day level, and they had not reached full capacity yet. A series of mysterious events began in 1906 for Tombstone Consolidated Mines Company when on January 11th the hoist for the Tranquility Mine caught fire destroying the structure and cracking the foundation. This mishap occurred when materials necessary to the further advancement of the Boom Shaft were delayed. Was the fire caused by the smoldering coal accidentally left unattended by a workman, which was the speculation, or was it deliberately set to avoid any layoffs while awaiting the arrival of the Boom Shaft materials? Since malice was not suspected, work continued at a furious pace to repair the damage. Later in 1906, Tombstone Consolidated Mines Company arbitrarily raised wages, which caught the town and the workers by surprise. In December of 1906, the Boom Shaft reached the 1000-foot level and work began immediately to cut out drifts for a new pumping station at this landmark depth.

In 1907 Tombstone Consolidated Mines Company would reach the pinnacle of achievement when the pumps at the 1000-foot level began running in June. However, it would realize the fragility of its venture in September when the prices in metals dropped severely, causing the company to lay off 50 miners on October 2nd. Still reeling from the cause and effect of the metals market, both the City and the Company maintained a pensive posture. On November 28, 1907 the hoist works of the Lucky Cuss Mine caught fire and was destroyed, the second mysterious catastrophe for

Tombstone Consolidated Mines Company. Fortunately for Tombstone Consolidated Mines Company, the shaft experienced little damage, but this structure was not insured. To defray expenses, the head frame, boiler and hoist were moved from the Toughnut Mine, but the Lucky Cuss would not get back into production until August of 1908.

The year 1908 provides a glimpse of life in Tombstone returning to "normal" in the new mining era. As in the earlier mining days, the populous of Tombstone valued their leisure time. When it was completed, Schieffelin Hall was the largest opera house between El Paso, Texas and San Francisco, California, and it was state of the art in its day. Magicians, theatrical ensembles and variety entertainers played to full houses when they performed at this venerable theatre. The restaurants of the 1880's offered culinary delicacies and wonders from all over the world, and the saloons provided the best spirits and games of chance. The level and quality of entertainment in Tombstone in 1908 was very similar to that in 1880, but in 1908, the citizenry had more genres to choose. There were not only live performers, there were moving pictures. What better venue to show this new wonder of the 20th Century than Schieffelin Hall. Many times live acts and movies were combined on the same bill to provide an evening of full entertainment for the patrons. As the year progressed, smaller theatres would open, but *"The Schieffelin"* would remain the center of entertainment from the comical to the cultural.

Restaurants and restaurateurs had changed, but many familiar names were still around. The Can Can and Russ House were two of the best eateries in Tombstone during the 1880's and they still were in 1908. The National was a relatively new bistro that looked to make its mark in Tombstone dining history. The menu for Christmas Dinner 1908 at The National follows on the next page with an ad for The Schieffelin's weekend bill.

THE SCHIEFFELIN.

Admission . . . . . 15 Cents

Mr. Hans Berndt.... Musical Director

Performances Promptly At 7:30 P. M

For Friday and Saturday Nights.

PROGRAM.

Moving Picture.
The Soldier's Dream.

Illustrated Song.
"In the Wildwood, Where the Blue Bell's Grow."
Miss Ellen Berndt.

Moving Picture.
The Bathers' Race.

Moving Picture,
The Pearl Fisher.

SPECIAL FEATURE.

Moving Picture
Blue Beard.

The Tombstone Prospector, January 3, 1903

The National Restaurant

CHAS. KREUDER, Mgr.

MENU

XMAS '03

Essence of Chicken a l'Ambassatrice
Canape's a la Gastronome
Guaymas Snapper a la Circassienne
Boiled Ox Tongue Sauce Chibolata
Roast Prime Beef au jus
Suckling Pig with Grenadine of Oranges
Roast Young Turkey, Chestnut Dressing and Cranberry Sauce
Oyster Patties a la Zingara
Salpicon of Turkey Livers with Mushrooms
Pork Tenderloin en Casserole a la Financiero
Mashed Potatoes
Baked Sweet Potatoes
Asparagus en Branche   French Peas
Green Apple Pie   Mince Pie
English Plum Pudding   Brandy Sauce
Roman Punch a la Cardinale
Cafe Noire
Fruit   Nuts
Christmas Cake
Cheese and Crackers

The Tombstone Prospector, December 23, 1903

The same year would find the work in the mines progressing very well. The panic of the previous year was seen as a mere hiccup. The pumps at the 1000-foot level were running smoothly, allowing miners to cut and expand drifts into new ore bodies. Life was good again in Tombstone until October of 1908. On the evening of October 7th another mysterious calamity struck Tombstone Consolidated Mines Company. Someone with explosives experience blew up one of the 15,000 gallon water tanks used by the mill. The pipeline was also destroyed and the townspeople were so incensed that had the perpetrator been found, there may have been a second lynching in Tombstone. The Tombstone Development Company, an offshoot of Tombstone Consolidated Mines Company, had been formed and supplied electricity, ice and water to the town. Their water tanks were near the one blown up. A rivalry had formed with the longstanding water supplier, The Huachuca Water Company, so it is not clear which was the intended target, Tombstone Consolidated Mines Company or Tombstone Development Company. Based on the expansion and production in mines, it does not seem logical that the mining company would be targeted for assault.

The Tombstone Prospector,
October 8, 1908

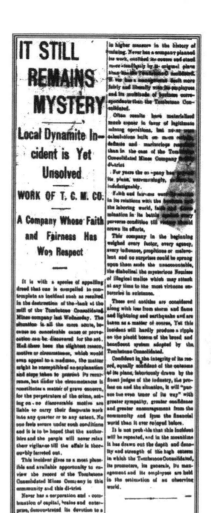

The Tombstone Prospector,
October 14, 1908

Tombstone Consolidated Mines Company immediately issued a $250 reward for the arrest and conviction of the guilty party. The notice, immediately published in the newspaper, inexplicably stops running after a matter of weeks, yet there is no report that the perpetrators were ever caught.

> # NOTICE.
> ## $250.00 Reward
> ---
> The above reward will be paid for the arrest and conviction of the party or parties who destroyed the water tank of this company on the night of October 7th.
> ## TOMBSTONE C. M. CO.

The Tombstone Prospector, October 1903

    Under the guidance of E.W. Walker, Tombstone Consolidated Mines Company's miners had achieved every goal set by management. However, Walker resigned his position as Superintendent at the end of December of 1908 to return home to Michigan. The announcement of his resignation was preceded in the newspaper with an article of cautious optimism for the coming year. Billy Hattich's prediction for 1909 was not as enthusiastic as the one from 1903. Hattich was simply looking back at the past and reminding his readers of the potential volatility of the precious metals market, but 1909 would not bring the erratic fluctuations in silver prices they had seen in 1907. It would bring the mysterious incident that would ultimately doom Tombstone Consolidated Mines Company.

The Tombstone Prospector, December 28, 1908   The Tombstone Prospector, December 30, 1908

James H. Macia took over as Superintendent for the Tombstone Consolidated Mines Company in January of 1909. A long time mining man, he had been brought in to help construct the Boom Shaft in Tombstone. The pumps were spewing out 6,000,000 gallons of water each day, and new pockets of rich ore were being uncovered daily. It appears as if 1909 would indeed be a banner year for the mines and for Tombstone. On the last day of May water somehow got into the fuel tanks of the boilers causing them to shut down. Without steam, the pumps stopped one by one. The pump men and miners were able to evacuate, but the water began to rise again. The lower stations were under water before the fires could be relit.

A MISHAP WHICH CAUSED TROUBLE

Water Crowds Lower Levels During an Accident But is Checkmated in Due Time

A SERIOUS DIFFICULTY IS PROMPTLY MET

Just how much of an important factor is steam to the successful operation of a colossal mining enterprise was perhaps never better illustrated than the lack of that powerful agency for a few brief hours at the big hoisting and pumping plant of the T. C. M. Co. yesterday morning.

A quantity of accrued water in an oil tank, accidentally permitted to flow into the feed pipes to the big boilers, caused the inevitable to happen and, temporarily, the mighty machinery became paralyzed, its effect being instantaneous. The big pumps became silent and helpless and the regular inflow of water on the 1,000-foot level, unchecked, began gradually to fill the station. Just here was illustrated in the few hours of time lost, the value of the essential force and potent power of steam, for in the lack of it caused the temporary upsetting of well laid systematic plans which will require several days to recover and will involve considerable expense and loss.

The water filled the lower station but the miners had ample time in which to reach points of safety. Yesterday four sinkers were installed to lower the water. Today two additional sinkers were connected and this afternoon the water is being perceptibly lowered, the mine management being hopeful of restoring conditions to normal within a few days.

"We do not regard the accident with alarm," said General Manager W. F. Staunton today in speaking of the situation, which reassurance is pleasing news to Tombstoners. Mr. Staunton paid a high tribute to the heroic work of the mechanics and force whose prompt service in installing sinkers to check the water was invaluable and a great aid in the task of recovering the station before the same assumed a more serious aspect.

This temporary suspension of the extraction of ore seems to weigh but lightly on the minds of Messrs. Gage and Staunton, who direct the necessary repairs in a methodical and philosophical manner and we have assurances that but a few days will elapse when the stamps will again be dropping at the mill and ore shipments will be the order of the day.

The Tombstone Prospector, June 1, 1909

Through the tenacity of James Macia and his men, the pumping stations were recovered, but not until Tombstone

Consolidated Mines Company had expended $500,000 (over $6,000,000 in current dollars) to repair the damage. This was money they could ill afford as the company was running short on cash at the time. A meeting of the Board of Directors was hastily summoned in Tombstone. Although they maintained a blasé public image concerning the "accident," the disaster could not have occurred at a worse time. Gage was determined that the company would never be put in this position again and designed a plan to install a second set of pumps on the 800 and the 1,000 foot levels.

MINING WORK ON THE HILL

New Machinery Expected This Month. Favorable Outlook for Extensive Exploration Work

OTHER MINES OF THE TOMBSTONE DISTRICT

It is expected that the supplemental pumping machinery and large air compressor for the Tombstone Consolidated Mines company will arrive here about the latter part of this month. Supt Mocia has the foundation work and 800-station level in shape to place the underground equipment while everything will be in readiness to start the general forward movement with the arrival of the additional machinery.

The present pumping record is in the neighborhood of 4,700,000 gallons per day which holds the water at the present level. The additional machinery will mean a 7,500,000 gallon record and with the recovery of the west on pump on the 1000 foot level a combined capacity of 10,000,000 gallons can easily be maintained, if required.

It will be noted that the extensive plans being followed are indicative of exploration work on a large scale and by the time 1910 rolls around Tombstone will be enjoying an increased era of prosperity.

While preparations are being made for new machinery, etc., the regular quota of ore is being shipped to the El Paso smelter and 40 stamps of the T C M Co mill kept grinding on ore.

At the Bunker Hill the work of reopening the property is well under way and during the month the first shipment will be started to the smelter. The ore from the Bunker Hill carries manganese and it is much in demand at the smelters.

The Tombstone Go'd, Silver & Copper company, under the management of J W Clark, is developing their properties and at present are sinking at the Ross group.

The Hershall company is maintaining their shipping record. Manager Douglas Grey is also extending development work and more rich strikes looked for in this admirable Tombstone producer.

The Tombstone Prospector, October 9, 1909

The plan was implemented, but Gage would not be there when his concept was tested. On November 12, 1909 at the Tombstone Consolidated Mines Company annual meeting, E.B. Gage resigned, citing health reasons as the cause. Frank Murphy replaced Gage as president. The people of Tombstone were devastated when Gage left. Despite his experience in mining, Murphy could not overcome the gloom that had beset Tombstone.

The Tombstone Prospector, November 10, 1909

In an attempt to calm the citizens of Tombstone, Hattich preceded the resignation article with the following:

The Tombstone Prospector, November 10, 1909

The news of the new equipment, as well as Macia's heroics, did little to soothe the loss of E.B. Gage.

Tombstone Consolidated Mines Company continued to fight for the survival into 1910. The battle now was not only the depth of the water but also the strength of the underground currents carrying the water. The deeper they went, the stronger the current. New boilers were brought in to generate more horsepower. Soon 6,500,000 gallons of water were flowing down the wash every day, but it was not enough. Each success was met with an equal or larger failure. On the fiscal side, the parent company of Tombstone Consolidated Mines Company, the Development Company of America, was having financial problems of its own. The Development Company of America had invested in too many other ventures besides the Tombstone mining operation. Struggles between management and stockholders continued throughout 1910, as did the struggle to produce more and more horsepower for the pumps. No agreement or resolution could be reached to recapitalize both ailing companies. On January 18, 1911 a telegram was delivered to the Tombstone Consolidated Mines Company office instructing the management to close the mines.

The Tombstone Prospector, January 18, 1911

Both companies soon field bankruptcy owing hundreds of thousands of dollars to suppliers and employees. That July, Frank Murphy placed $40,000 in an account to pay all back wages and accounts in Tombstone with interest. The bankruptcy proceeding would linger on until May 16, 1914, when the meeting of creditors unanimously voted to sell the Tombstone Consolidated Mines Company property at public auction.

TOMBSTONE HAS BRIGHT FUTURE

Sale of T. C. M. Co. Properties Will be Effected at Early Date---History of Bankrupt Case

MEETING OF CREDITORS HELD HERE SATURDAY

Will Sell Properties

At the meeting of creditors of the Tombstone Consolidated Mines Company, bankrupt, held Saturday in the Company Offices building, and called by Referee in Bankruptcy Daniel McFarland, for the purpose of passing on the petition of creditors on sale of the properties en masse. The petition was granted at the hearing before Referee McFarland and the date of the sale, while not definitely fixed, will take place sometime next month.

Big Companies Interested

Thus, from the above, it may be noted that the formal legal steps looking to the final adjudication of the local bankruptcy have been taken. The sale, after being advertised, will take place before when the date is fixed and that some big company will take the situation in hand to the best interests of the community is assured. The Copper Queen company of Bisbee, famed for its big undertakings and success in the mining world, is looking over the local field, and, it is understood, will bid hard for the properties. It is reported that several other companies have been looking over the properties, and much interest is centered on the final outcome.

Employ Many Men

But the fact that the properties are to be sold in the near future fortells that the Old Camp is to come to its own again and the reopening of the workings and the prospecting of virgin fields, that are known to contain millions of valuable ore, will again give employment to an army of men in the famous old district.

The properties, except for the work of chloriders, have remained idle for the past several years, 'tis true, but the delay has been caused by the courts and proceedings in the bankruptcy matter.

History of the Case

When the company first went into bankruptcy all claims against the company were allowed by Referee McFarland, with the exception of certain bonds issued by the company in the amount of about three million dollars which were declared to be not valid claims against the bankrupt concern, inasmuch as was stated upon the face

The Tombstone Prospector, May 18, 1914

Naturally rumors began to fly all over Tombstone about who the new owners might be. The Guggenheim family has extensive holdings in Arizona, as did Phelps-Dodge Company. Both has engineers inspect and report on the mines. The ever optimistic Hattich continued to "spin" the status of Tombstone Consolidated Mines company's holdings and the fate of Tombstone itself.

BIG MINE SALE HERE TOMORROW

Trustee Col. A. L. Grow Will Sell Entire Holdings of Bankrupt Company—Many Interested

EXPECTED THAT MILLIONS WILL BE INVOLVED

Tomorrow, Tuesday, June 23rd, at 10:00 a.m., on the court house steps of Cochise county, Trustee A L Grow of the Tombstone Consolidated Mines Company, Bankrupt, will offer for sale at public auction, the entire property of the bankrupt estate, to the highest bidder.

The sale will include all the mines, machinery and everything owned by the bankrupt company. The mammoth pumping plant, air compressor, the gigantic boilers, installed just before the mine was closed; the ponderous hoisting machinery, as well as the railroad and milling equipment and the various shafts such as the Tribute, Tranquility, Silver Thread, and others too numerous to mention, which, together with the main shaft the Boom, have, during the operation of the company, produced fabulous millions in gold, silver and copper ore. But the immense volume of water encountered on the 1000 foot level several years ago, coupled with the many millions that had to be expended in combating the enormous flow, resulted in the company going into bankruptcy.

Since that time much has taken place. The case has been in the courts most of the time, and was only recently cleared when the Supreme Court at Washington, after the case had gone through all the procedure from the Referee, upheld the decision of Referee Daniel McFarland, that the million dollar bond issue could not be held as valid claims against the bankrupt company. Matters could then take their course, and subsequently Trustee Col A L Grow issued the call for bids on the property en masse, and designated the 23rd day of June as the day of sale. Col Grow, as trustee, has conducted the affairs of the estate in a most excellent manner. The property has been self-sustaining under his management, and not once, throughout the entire three years, during which time only leasing on a small scale was done on the properties, has it been necessary to issue trustee's certificates, which is customary in all big cases of this kind, and which speaks highly of the able manner in which Mr Grow has handled the matter.

Since the company went into bankruptcy, many thousands have been produced by the lessors, and this without extensive work, which goes to show that there still lies in this district, the precious metals which lured thousands into the golden west.

No doubt with the sale tomorrow of the entire properties of the Tombstone Consolidated Mines Company, by Trustee Grow, Tombstone will have entered in on a new era of prosperity. For if the property falls into the hands of a big reliable company, as is expected, the prediction has been made that it will not be long before the Old Camp will again be numbered among the thriving mining cities of the southwest.

The sale is awaited with great interest both here and elsewhere, and no doubt tomorrow will see a large number at the court house when the sale takes place. The notice and full description of the property may be seen on page four of this issue of the Prospector, and will make interesting reading.

The Tombstone Prospector, June 22, 1914

Finally on June 23, 1914, a large crowd gathered in the courtroom of the Cochise County Courthouse in Tombstone for this monumental event. A.L. Grow, the appointed Trustee, proclaimed the bidding would begin, but the room fell silent. Out of the crowd, Walter Douglas, the General Manager of Phelps-Dodge, declared a bid of $500,000. No other bids were made.

The Tombstone Prospector, June 23, 1914

After the mandatory ten-day waiting period, the sale was consummated. The Tombstone mines now belonged to Phelps-Dodge Company, and the town was rejuvenated with the hope that operations would begin again.

T.C.M. COMPANY SALE TO DOUGLAS IS CONFIRMED

At Meeting of Creditors Held Today In Tombstone

NO PLANS AS YET

The sale of the Tombstone Consolidated Mines Company properties to Walter Douglas, was confirmed today at the meeting of the creditors, in the T. C. M. Company offices, held for the purpose of confirmation this afternoon. This marks the last step in the transformation of the property to the purchaser, Walter Douglas, and the property will now be transferred to him.

While nothing definite has as yet been given out by Mr. Douglas, it is generally reported that long time leases are to be given out to those who desire, and the old workings will be worked in this matter, while prospecting will be carried on in different parts of the district It is generrlly conceded also that Dr E Grebe, will have charge of the entire holdings here as general manager and superintendent, but so far no definite plan has been learned, as to which course will be pursued, although it is expected that an announcement will be forthcoming soon.

The Tombstone Prospector, July 6, 1914

Thus began the Phelps-Dodge mining era in Tombstone. As the article states, the company did lease out many of the properties acquired in the purchase of the Tombstone Consolidated Mines Company holdings. They relocated the company office to E.B. Gage's home located among the mining works on Empire Hill. From here, Dr. Emil Grebe, the Phelps-Dodge Superintendent for Tombstone would guide the region in a new direction.

CHAPTER SIXTEEN

The continent of Europe was thrown into war just days before Walter Douglas bid for the Tombstone Consolidated Mines Company property. This tragedy created a need for a different mineral that the Tombstone Hills were rich in, manganese. Although the boys of Cochise County and Tombstone did more than their fair share in the fighting, it was this resource that most aided the Allies in World War I. Grebe immediately directed that work in the Bunker Hill Mine be focused on manganese. In 1916 it was reported that some 400 miners were working the Tombstone Hills and by 1917 the number swelled to 600. At its peak, 90% of the manganese mined for the war effort was coming from Tombstone. Of course this was in addition to the lead and silver that the mines continued to produce. Tombstone continued to prosper until the war ended in spite of the increased regulation of mines and mining. When the fighting ended, so did the need for mass quantities of manganese. On March 18, 1918, **The Prospector** reported that work in the Bunker hill Mine had been ordered to stop.

After the war the United States Congress passed the Pittman Act. The Pittman Act was a United State federal law sponsored by Senator Key Pittman of Nevada and enacted on April 23, 1919. The act authorized the conversion of, not exceeding, 350,000,000 standard silver dollars into bullion, and its sale, or use for subsidiary silver coinage. It directed purchase of domestic silver for recoinage of a like number of a like number of dollars. Just as the demand for manganese was decreasing, this legislature breathed a new life into the price of silver in a global way. For Tombstone, as they said in the 1880s, "the ball was open," and silver was "king". Unlike Tombstone Consolidated Mines Company, Phelps-Dodge took a much more conservative approach to business. They never attempted to lower the water level in all of the mines. They maximized the existing drifts and stopes. The management chose to work the Tombstone mines at a much more methodical manner, and it paid huge dividends.

Since the Pittman Act was solely intended to bolster the world economy until foreign currencies could be stabilized, Tombstone again became victim to the volatility of an open market on silver prices. On May 31, 1923 the Treasury Department announced the suspension of the Pittman Act.

> ## Orders Do Not Call For Complete Shut-Down of Bunker Hill Properties in Tombstone
>
> MANY RUMORS, UNFOUNDED, SPREAD ABOUT COUNTY; DEVELOPMENT WORK AND LEASES WILL STILL BE PROSECUTED BY THE COMPANY; MANY BELIEVE ORDER TEMPORARY; FORSEE GREATER THINGS.
>
> Coming as a complete surprise to the management as well as the public of Tombstone, the orders came yesterday to suspend operations, on production work, on the local Bunker Hill Mines company's properties. Since that time the matter has been the subject of much discussion and rumors, but up until late this afternoon as far as could be learned the orders do not call for a complete shutdown of all the properties of the Bunker Hill workings in Tombstone, as previously reported.
>
> Through a semi-official channel it is learned that the orders do not call for a complete suspension, but it is known that a small force of men are to be kept at work at the Oregon and other manganese-silver properties doing development and exploration work, and completing the tunnels that were started some time ago to tap the Oregon to facilitate shipment of ore. The power house and machine shops are also to be continued, while leases are to be given out on all gold and silver properties, excluding manganese, the local public drawing the natural inference that the company intends to hold the manganese for future production work. This is also sustained by the report that the Phelps-Dodge company, of which the Bunker Hill is a subsidiary, has been making exhaustive tests for a process to extract both the manganese and silver contents from the local ore, the silver heretofore having been a loss and which, if extracted, would have completely paid for handling. It is also reported that the Phelps-Dodge are to start construction of a mammoth concentrator at Warren similar to the one at Miami, in which all ores from Bisbee and manganese from Tombstone is to be reduced, thereby saving both silver and manganese values in the Tombstone ores.
>
> Speculation and street talk has been rife all through today as to what the company was to do and what they were not to do, and many spelled the doom of Tombstone, while others see a possibly brighter future pointing out the various circumstances surrounding the orders, and drawing natural conclusions.
>
> But the matter narrows down to the point where local people should not believe reports that are unfounded, and look hopefully for the best, even though today matters seem to be slightly adverse. It is known that the ore is here, and that this is one of the largest manganese fields in the United tSates according to the report of Dr. F. L. Ransome, of the U. S. Geological Survey, who recently made his report, and this being the true facts, the United States government needs the precious metal too badly at present during war times to warrant a complete discontinuance of production. All of which leads the local optimistic residents to believe that the shutdown is only temporary.
>
> As far as present orders go, all production work will be closed by April 1st., leaving open only leases and development work.
>
> Telephone conversations with the general offices of the Phelps-Dodge at Bisbee late this afternoon disclosed nothing futher than that, stating that there was nothing further for publication.

The Tombstone Prospector, March 23, 1918

U. S. Treasury Suspends Silver Act Purchases

WASHINGTON, May 30.—Announcement was made by the treasury tonight of a suspension of silver purchases under the Pittman act, until it can be determined definitely whether the estimates of offers already exceed the 200,000,000 ounces which the law authorized the government to buy.

The announcement means that the government has practically completed another phase of its war time financing through the replacement of almost all of the silver loaned to Great Britain in 1918 to stave off a threatened rebellion in India. It means also, officials believe, that the treasury will be out of the silver market as a buyer except for immaterial mounts for several years.

The Tombstone Prospector, May 31, 1923

The next day, a detailed account of this action was published in The Prospector:

U. S. TREASURY ANNOUNCEMENT ON PITTMAN ACT

That the Treasury announcement does not mean the completion of the Pittman Act, is the gist of telegraphic advices received in Tombstone today from J. F. Galbraith, secretary of the American Mining Congress, in reply to a wire sent him on the 30th by A. M. Morris, superintendent of the Bunker Hill Mines Company. In his wire Mr. Galbraith said:

"Treasury announcement does not mean completion of the Pittman Act. All tenders made to close of business Tuesday, May 29th were received and accepted. Beginning this morning tenders will be received but acceptances will be held in abeyance until exact amount purchasable can be definitely ascertained."

The quantity of silver remaining purchasable by the government under the Pittman Act is approximately 1,000,000 ounces according to the latest advices received here, although in previous reports amounts purchasable were given as 5,000,000 on May 19th, 6,000,000 on the 22rd, 5,000,000 on the 25th and on the 29th the Treasury Department announced suspension of purchases pending a check of purchases to determine the amount yet to be secured under the act. The result of the check should be made public by tomorrow, according to advices received here, and if the balance to be purchased under the act remains at around 1,000,000, the purchases under the act will consume not more than two or three days, if tenders are made at the rate of the past few days in May, which ranged between 200,000 and 400,000 ounces per day, according to a recent bulletin.

It is probable that in order to protect local shippers, the smelters will immediately go to provisional settlement pending the securing of definite data from the mint of the status of purchases under the Pittman Act.

This announcement should be made not later than tomorrow, and will probably be issued today.

Relative to the silver situation a recent silver bulletin notes the fact that Under-Secretary Gilbert, of the Treasury, is expected to reaffirm his decision not to purchase the 14,500,000 ounces of silver under the Pittman Act at $1 per ounce, which was used for subsidiary coinage and which Senator Pittman contends should be replaced.

"It is not a healthy condition for any industry to be hanging on the ragged edge," declared Sen. Oddie, Republican, of Nevada, chairman of the Senate Gold and Silver Commission. "Consumers of silver in the arts will be in much better condition if we have a healthy and normal silver production in this country. The Commission is trying to get something started which will stimulate the price of silver, or in other words keep it up to a proper level. Whether we can accomplish it in time to prevent even a temporary slump in the price of silver which may occur when purchases under the Pittman Act at $1 per ounce are terminated, remains to be seen. The commission believes,

(Continued on Page Two)

TREASURY ANNOUNCEMENT ON PITTMAN ACT.

(Continued from Page One)

however, that if the right step can be taken, the price of silver can be maintained at a proper level."

The Commission is making a study of producing, marketing and distributing associations as a basis for some plan of orderly and concentrated marketing of silver in order to maintain the price at a figure to insure silver producers a fair profit.

Data is also being collected by the Commission to be submitted to a meeting of silver producers to be held at Reno, during the summer, probably in August, at which the commission will consider plans to stabilize and improve the price of silver through a silver export association or some other plan. To this meeting will be invited all American silver producers who are interested in properties in North, South and Central America, Canada, the United States and Mexico, who are said to represent 90 per cent of the world's silver production. The Commission will also seek the views of the silver producers on proposed legislation in the interest of the silver mining industry.

John Hays Hammond, mining engineer, considers it important to stabilize the price of silver and believes the Senate Gold and Silver Commission will be helpful in bringing this about. He favors combination of silver producers in order to maintain the price at a figure to assure a fair profit over cost of production but is said to feel that the only drawback to such a combination would be the unwillingness of smelting companies who handle silver as a by-product to hold their silver at a higher price as it could be sold cheaper by being a by-product, and because of the further fact that it would involve considerable money to finance a holding corporation. Mr. Hammond also says that the lead industry has a great future.

The Tombstone Prospector, June 1, 1923

Phelps-Dodge had covertly shifted its focus to leasing the mines in the Tombstone Hills. After the repeal of the Pittman Act, only a few independent lessees continued to work the claims that had been made famous some forty-five years earlier, but they would never realize the wealth their predecessors had known.

Tombstone would again try to resurrect itself beginning in 1929 with the first Helldorado Days. Walter Noble Burns, Frederick Bechdolt, Billy Breakenridge and John Clum had all penned books about Tombstone's glorious beginnings. Americans started to visit Tombstone to see the "Old West" before it was gone. William Kelly, owner and editor of the ***Tombstone Epitaph*** newspaper, conceived the idea of Helldorado Days, but like its mining fortunes this too would fall prey to the stock market. The first day of Helldorado Days in 1929 was October 24th, "Black Thursday," when the stock market crashed. But Tombstone would find its new niche, tourism, following the advent of movies and television focusing on the legends Wyatt Earp, Cochise County and Tombstone. It is important to state that there are <u>still</u> miles of silver, gold and other minerals buried in those shafts from 1878, but Mother Nature's aquifer has reclaimed them once again.

The hoist works and boilers are all gone. Today the hills over Tombstone lay quiet as homes and apartments replace mills and water tanks, but the glorious history still remains, that during both mining bonanzas, Tombstone was the toast of the silver mining boom towns.

Dormant Mine Works circa 1930's
Author's Collection

CHAPTER SEVENTEEN

In 1929, Tombstone, Arizona had become a mere shell of the thriving city it once had been. From 1879 to 1889, Tombstone had been the pinnacle of mining boom towns. After the price of silver dropped, the mines all but closed down. In 1902 when E.B. Gage reopened 90% of the mines, the city experienced a renaissance. This period of prosperity would end in 1923 when silver prices dropped again. A few mines remained in operation, but nowhere near the scale of the previous decades. The small economic surge created by the need for lead and manganese during World War I had subsided. The notoriety achieved during the Wobblie deportation trials had past. And the impact of Frederick Bechdolt's articles and books was waning. Yet thanks to the historians of the day, the residents of Tombstone were beginning to see the potential of a new "industry" for their community, tourism. Walter Noble Burns' *Tombstone, An Illiad of the Southwest,* along with Bechdolt's works, had created a public interest in visiting the sire so rich in the history of the Old West. The community was also facing another crisis. Bisbee and Douglas were strong, prosperous copper-mining cities that coveted Tombstone's designation as the Cochise County Seat.

William Kelly, the editor of the Tombstone Epitaph newspaper, had been born and raised in Cochise County so he knew its history well. His father, George H. Kelly, had taken over the paper three years earlier, but by 1929 his focus was on his position as State Historian. The spring of 1929 was like every other spring. The County Fairs were held, as were many annual local festivities around Tombstone. Kelly advertised them all in his paper. It seemed as though every nearby locale had some event to attract visitors and entertain the residents. However, Tombstone offered no such activity. William realized that this year would be the fiftieth anniversary of the founding of Tombstone, and he believed that the town should mark this occasion with an even grand enough to reflect its glory days. Kelly would embellish the plan to include the 50th anniversary of the Tombstone Epitaph newspaper, and he acknowledged that this aspect was one year premature. The best person to tell the story of the phenomenal undertaking, in the author's opinion, is William Kelly. Many of his articles and editorials have been reproduced in this work to properly convey the magnitude of this undertaking, the accomplishments and the near successful retention of the County Seat in Tombstone.

On June 6, 1929, William Kelly published the following editorial outlining Tombstone's decline, and suggestions that the city launch a new era and new industry, tourism, with a "semi-centennial" celebration. Kelly also touted the climate and environment as assets that could attract a health sanitarium. After all, Tombstone had something none of the other communities had, national recognized history. He cited the years of publicity the town had received because of its early days, and went on to say that this event could serve as a springboard into Tombstone's future development. This fertile "seed" would blossom in a mere 4 ½ months into an once-in-a-lifetime extravaganza.

LET'S HAVE THAT CELEBRATION

Just fifty years ago this spring the first miners, store-keepers, freighters, saloon men and gamblers were erecting their temporary and unsightly frame and adobe shacks along the present streets of Tombstone.

Since early in the year of 1879 the roads and trails from Silver City, Tucson, El Paso and Sonora had been crowded with teams and pack trains bringing the first citizens and their belongings to what was destined to become the greatest silver camp of the early 80's All summer long the building up of this new town continued and seemingly overnight the surrounding country became dotted with the white tents of prospectors, adventurers, miners and the conglomeration of citizenry that went to make up a mushroom camp. By fall the town had taken on some semblance of order. Saloons and dance halls were running full blast. Freighters, mounted cowboys, buckboards and pack trains crowded the main streets. A. E. Fay and Thomas Tully had started the Tombstone Nugget, the first newspaper, and on the hill several hundred miners were opening up the Contention, the Lucky Cuss, the Emerald, the Silver Thread and other claims and Tombstone silver was just reaching the world silver market. John Ringo, Curly Bill, Buckskin Frank Leslie, the Clantons, the McLowerys, the Earps, Doc Holiday, Breakenridge, Ed Vail and others who were to shine brightly in the spotlight of Tombstone were just beginning to arrive.

The whole story is one of the most romantic and interesting ones in the history of the west. It has inspired the publication of four books and perhaps thousands of newspaper stories and magazine articles. It is a story of pioneering, hardship, recklessness and quick riches.

A half century has passed since these events transpired and Tombstone is entering a new era in the history of its development. Climate, scenery and the attraction of the great outdoors will take the place of silver and gold. Thousands of Americans seeking these things will find them at their best in Tombstone and it is not hard to visualize the day when this city will again come into its own.

What could be more fitting than to introduce the new period in the history of Tombstone with a celebration commemorating its establishment. The thousands of people who have read these books and magazine articles have promised themselves a trip here. The publicity surrounding an event of this kind together with the wide-spread publicity the town has already received would undoubtedly attract both the visitor and the investor. A new hotel, new homes, possibly a sanitarium would inevitably follow. The time is ripe, the opportunity is present and the task is not beyond our capabilities.

COURTESY OF THE TOMBSTONE EPITAPH NEWSPAPER
JUNE 6, 1929

The following week, in Tombstone's bustling neighbor, Bisbee, carried this editorial:

TOMBSTONE'S CELEBRATION

The Bisbee Daily Review in their editorial column yesterday morning had the following to say regarding the celebration of Tombstone's Fiftieth Anniversary.

The editorial as printed by the Review is a fair indication of the enthusiasm expressed by nearly every one who has given the possibilities of a thing of this kind any consideration.

"Tombstone is discussing the possibilities of commemorating the fiftieth anniversary of the founding of that romantic city with a three or four day celebration in which the county seat would again take on the appearance of the romantic mining camp of the early eighties. But why discuss it, why not start immediately to lay plans for the greatest celebration ever attempted in the west The possibilities are unlimited. No city in America has had the publicity which has been accorded Tombstone during the past few years; no city in America has preserved so many old landmarks; no city in America has preserved so many of the old landmarks that are connected with its romantic past. The expenditure of a few thousand dollars and Tombstone could be changed back to the mining camp of 1880, with its rows of saloons and gambling houses, its Bird-Cage theater and Crystal Palace. Incidents of the early Days—the Earp feud—could be re-enacted in their original surroundings, and the Bird Cage could be reopened for a variety show. There is no limit to the size and quality of the entertainment that could be worked up with the assistance of the few old timers who are still with us, and with the proper advertising a celebration of this kind would draw people from every part of the country."

COURTESY OF THE TOMBSTONE EPITAPH NEWSPAPER
JUNE 13, 1929

Two weeks later, Tucson added their "two cents" in support of Kelley's plan. The reaction from the surrounding communities was overwhelmingly positive. It almost seemed as though the Arizonans in and around the area were falling under Kelly's spell. They too wanted to see, touch and feel Tombstone in its heyday. They wanted to live and walk in the history of Tombstone and the Old West.

Editorial

TOMBSTONE'S SEMI-CENTENNIAL.

Tombstone is discusing a proposal to formally celebrate the semi-centennial of its founding. Fifty years ago is no great age for a city to have atained, and compared with Tucson the county capital of Cochise has no more than reached the gosling age, but in terms of change it might have been founded five hundred years ago. It lives in the mellow light of romance, not only for its dwellers but for its wandering sons. These were formerly so many, so adventurous, and so widespread that each week Bill Hattich was enabled to announce some sensational feat accomplished by a "former Tombstoner." Every Telegraphed news story telling of an unusual accomplishment—from the climbing of a porch to the climbing of a hitherto unscaled precipice—was susceptible of localization, for all adventurers it was suspected, must at some time have tarried at Tombstone. Thus "old Tombstoners" each week brought to Editor and Publisher Bill Hattich rich cargo of sensation and amazement; the news mills of the wide world poured a steady stream of grist into the Epitaph's hopper.

Tucson and Tombstone are closely linked in history and Cochise capital may count on the sympathetic patronage of Old Pueblo if it determines to celebrate its semi-centennial. — Tucson Citizen.

COURTESY OF THE TOMBSTONE EPITAPH NEWSPAPER
JUNE 27, 1929

Mayor Ray B. Krebs, an automobile salesman and later insurance salesman, recognized the "hook" Kelly described in his editorial. He realized that such an extravaganza could restore the luster of Tombstone's importance in and to Cochise County. In June of 1929, he and the city Council unanimously approved Kelly's proposal to spearhead the gala, with the Epitaph providing the funding in return for 60% of the profits. Krebs personally contributed $1,000.00 toward the event. In three short weeks, his idea had become the celebration Kelly hoped would breathe life into his home town again. On its face, Kelly's dream appeared to be simply a commemoration of the founding of Tombstone. In reality it was a masterful design to reassert Tombstone's significance in and to Cochise County. For years the town had fended off attempts to relocate the County Seat. Now in 1929, "the town too tough to die" faced a new "challenger," Douglas. Douglas was growing and prospering from copper mining. Bisbee had long been the center of copper mining, but Douglas was up and coming. The three County Supervisors, one of whom resided in Douglas, were beginning to publicly "leak" their intention to relocate the County Seat to Douglas. Kelly feared that this would be the death knell for Tombstone if the county Supervisors succeeded with their scheme. So Kelly's plan was to showcase Tombstone, in all of its glory, on a city, county, state and even national level. He hoped that the magnitude of the event and the sentiment that it would stir, would sway the vote in Tombstone's favor.

THE COURT HOUSE QUESTION

The very important question as to whether the people of Cochise County shall remove the county seat to some other point in the county will probably be brought up for decision again this fall.

The decision should be an economic one and a vote, yes or no, should be cast by the voters of the county only after a careful consideration of the immediate and subsequent costs of the move and whether or not the move is worth this cost to the taxpayers.

At this time the people of Tombstone are asking but one thing of the remainder of the county. We ask that they guard against any decision on this question based on malicious rumor, false information, unjust criticism or high pressure salesmanship. An example of this is the unfair and uncalled for report that Tombstone, the county seat, is without a doctor. It is true that sickness has robbed us of one of our doctors and that another has seen fit to transfer his office to an adjacent town. This condition, however, continued but for a day or two and at the present time an entirely capable physician has established an office here.

For close to fifty years Tombstone has been the county seat of Cochise County. During that time unfortunate circumstances have reduced this place from its position as Arizona's greatest city to a very small community. The handful of business men and others who will be forced to depend on honest judgment and unbiased house will not be able to pour a great deal of money into a slush fund to carry on this fight or to hire a skilled outside manager to take charge of the campaign. We will be forced to depend on honest judgment and unbased decision of the people of this county to keep the court house where it rightfully belongs and for this reason we again ask the people of the county to maintain an open mind and to consider this question solely on its merits.

COURTESY OF THE TOMBSTONE EPITAPH NEWSPAPER
SEPTEMBER 5, 1929

With the City Fathers behind him, Kelly called upon the citizens of Tombstone to become a part of Helldorado Days. He published the overall plan in the newspaper June 27th of 1929. He strategically reminded his fellow citizens of the impact the mere mention of the name "Tombstone" generates in the public's mind. Kelly also reminded them that this was their opportunity to establish a new "industry" in Tombstone. The city's history could become the new "mother lode" that would carry Tombstone's economy into the future. By becoming the icon of the old west, the city would be able to continue to be the only County Seat in Cochise County history. Kelly contented that the townspeople could transform the city into the symbol of the American West on their own. He continued his pitch, stating that by staging historic reenactments, bringing back pioneers of the day, exhibiting artifacts of the day against the backdrop of Tombstone, then "the show will be Tombstone."

ANNOUNCE HELLDORADO

SHOW TO BE GIVEN HERE TO CELEBRATE TOMBSTONE'S

FIFTIETH ANNIVERSARY!!

Scenes And Events Of Early History Will Be Re-enacted Here For

THOUSANDS OF VISITORS!!

"Tombstone's Helldorado," a city wide show of old time scenes and historic events will be given here next October by the city council and the citizens of Tombstone to celebrate the fiftieth anniversary of the founding of this place, according to an official announcement made by members of the council and other interested citizens this week.

The most interesting and dramatic pages in the history of this city will be re-enacted for the benefit of thousands of visitors. Nothing will be spared, according to the sponsors of the show, to present for a few short days a true to life picture of Tombstone as it appeared in the heyday of its glory.

The show will be Tombstone - - - the scene will be Tombstone and the entire town will live once more in the scenes and atmosphere of 1879. So far as possible modern improvements will be removed or covered over.

In the many original buildings still standing will be re-enacted the scenes and activities that made up the daily lives of such men as Ed Schieffelin, Wyatt Earp, John Ringo, Ike and Billy Clanton, Doc Holliday, Buckskin Frank Leslie, Bat Masterson, and the twenty others whose residence in Tombstone gave fame to this place.

The doors of the Bird Cage Theater, locked for more than 40 years, will again swing open to a crowded Allen Street. The old time variety performers and dance hall girls will once more make lively this sole remaining relic of a pioneer saloon and theater. The old dumb-waiter from the bar on the first floor to the boxes above will once more rattle with the load of drinks just sold by the commission girls and in the small hours of the morning when the last performer has finished his act the benches on the main floor will again be cleared and, as was the custom fifty years ago, the night will end in an old-time dance.

'At the Crystal Palace Bar - - Arizona's greatest saloon and gambling hall and the town's most popular meeting place - - - will again be enacted the life of a typical western mining camp. Saloons, restraunts, bowling alleys, hotels and stores - - - most of them vacant now - - will be repaired and re-furnished for the occasion and on the streets and in these buildings the people of Tombstone are determined to once more bring back the atmosphere and the lively events of an almost forgotten era in the development of this place.

It is the plan of the city council to block off the streets necessary for this performance and to hold the entire show within the limits of the present business district. Some of the present vacant buildings will be used for the showing of mining exhibits, pioneer exhibits and old Tombstone exhibits. Others will be made into old time saloons and dance halls and in others will be housed the various carnival and entertainment attractions that will go to make up the celebration. To hold the interest of the crowd and to make the show more lively it is possible that arrangements can be made to build a large platform just south of Allen Street on Fifth Street where at regular intervals high class performers will entertain the crowd. Here also will be held one of the old time rock drilling contests and to complete the picture the once famous volunteer fire department of this city will hold a hose cart race down Allen Street.

The big event of the show, however, will probably be the morning parade. In this parade will be shown, in pageant form, the development and growth of Tombstone and Arizona from the discovery of the mines here by Ed Schieffelin in modern times. Leading the parade, according to present plans, will be Ed Scheiffelin and his burro, loaded for a trip into the hills. This will be followed by Apache Indians, cowboys, soilders, covered wagons, miners, prospectors, the old stage coaches, ox teams, freight teams, old time buggies and the other characters and equipment that passed from one year to the next through the streets of Tombstone.

Merchants now doing business on the main street will be asked to help in the task of covering over the modern fronts, fixtures and signs that now how and to reconstruct in as true a manner as possible the appearance of these buildings as they were in the early days. Markers will be put up to identify the location of historic places and along Allen Street dirt will be thrown over the pavement to complete the picture.

Thousands of persons over the country who have read of Tombstone will not miss this opportunity to see it at its best and it is the hope of the city council to give them a show that will not be remembered. As an extra guarantee of success they have decided to bring a competent show man and organizer here far in advance of the celebration to direct the entertainment features and to work out the details of the program.

Living here in Tombstone it is hard for local residents to realize the tremendous attraction this place holds for eastern people or those who have recently come to Arizona from the east. The town and all its history spells romance and high adventure to these people. The Saturday Evening Post, Liberty, and other great national weeklies have told the story of Tombstone in their pages and recently the mere mention of this place to one of the editors of the New York Times brought forth a long editorial in that paper. When Wyatt Earp died this winter in California every paper in the United States carried all the information they could obtain regarding this early day peace officer and the town in which he gained his fame. Even in Paris the story of his death was carried under large headlines. It is this same attraction that will draw people from every section of the country during the celebration and, in the opinion of members of the city council, it will undoubtedly be the turning point in the efforts of local people to capitalize the scenic, historic and climatic attractions of this place.

Celebration Comments

J E. CAVANAUGH— "I think the celebration will be a fine thing for the town if those in charge have the cooperation of everybody."

MRS. NELLIE LEMMONS—"I think it is fine and hope that we can secure some of the old articles like the Shoder Stage and other relics."

LEM HILTON—"It will be a knockout as a publicity scheme for the town and may enable us to get a hotel and plenty of tourist trade."

L. G. FAHNESTOCK—"If the celebration is in accordance with the large history of the place it will be a boon to this town and I think all of Arizona should endorse and back the project."

OSCAR LILLYBECK—"As planned it will be a wonderful thing and many tourists on the way to their various homes will be attracted to the event. I don't doubt that many from the east will make special trips to be present at the time."

CHARLIE SANDERS—"If this celebration is to be put on at all it must be put on in the right manner. The possibilities are too great and a wonderful opportunity will be wasted if we do not get off to a good start with this. I believe that all the business men in Tombstone will be behind this thing and will do anything in their power to put it over."

P. M SODERSTROM—"There is not another place in the world more admirably situated to give a show of this kind. Hundreds and hundreds of people have been waiting for just such a chance to come here to Tombstone and when they come and see what we have to offer some of them are going to come back for more before very long."

COURTESY OF THE TOMBSTONE EPITAPH NEWSPAPER
JUNE 27, 1929

Throughout 1929, William Kelly printed weekly updates on the progress of the gala. He also reprinted articles and pieces from the archives of the Epitaph. Then, as it still is today, controversy arose concerning the deeds and effects of the 28 months the Earp brothers had lived in Tombstone between December of 1879 and April of 1882. This period of Tombstone history remains indistinguishable between legend and reality even today. One fact that can be used to clarify these two positions is that the Earp brothers appear to have been supported by the corporate/mining concerns, while the "Cowboys," as the outlaws called themselves; were supported by the meat marketers and ranchers. Wells Fargo & Company and the mining magnates of the day, the Earps' strongest supporters were long gone. However, many of the ranching families were still in the area, and they took great exception with the record according to the Epitaph, and they expressed their version of the events in letters to the paper.

ARGUMENT OVER EARP CHARACTER IS LIVELY ONE

Question of Just How Bad Early Peace Officer Was Is Subject of Letter

COURTESY OF THE TOMBSTONE EPITAPH NEWSPAPER
APRIL 25, 1929

171

Many of the details still needed to be worked out. The idea of Helldorado was firmly entrenched in the minds of the Tombstone residents. However, the development from concept to reality had to be carefully designed to achieve the intended success. A community wide meeting was announced on July 25, 1929, to be held the following Monday.

MAYOR KREBS IN CHARGE OF MASS MEETING MONDAY

Citizens All Asked To Meet For Discussion Of Helldorado

EVERYONE IS INVITED

Crystal Theater Is The Place; 7:30 P. M. Is The Time

A general mass meeting of all the citizens of Tombstone has been called for next Monday night at 7:30 o'clock at the Crystal theater by R. B. Krebs, mayor, for the purpose of going over the proposed plans for "Tombstone's Helldorado," a celebration to commemorate the Fiftieth Anniversary of the City of Tombstone, to be sponsored by the city council.

At a meeting of the council held last Wednesday night it was definitely decided by that body to sponsor the show and to call on the citizens of Tombstone to get behind the project and make it the greatest thing of its kind ever attempted in Arizona. Committee members from among the civic, social and business organizations of the city to handle the various departments of the show will be named at the meeting on Monday night.

It was announced by the council at this meeting that an attempt will be made to organize the show in such a way as to make it self supporting but that they have been successful in having the expenses of the enterprise adequately underwritten. This does away with one of the greatest problems confronting a celebration of this kind. It was also announced at this meeting that more than 40 lots in the business district of the city had been secured for use during the celebration and that these lots contained some of the most historic buildings in the city including the Bird Cage Theater.

It is the present plan of the council to hold the entire show within the business district of the town on Allen Street between Sixth and Fourth
(Turn To Page Four)

MAYOR KREBS—

(Continued from Page One)

and on Fifth Street between Allen and Fremont. This area will be blocked off and closed to traffic and all the buildings and property on these streets, so far as is possible, will be redecorated to resemble the appearance of the buildings standing there in the eighties. In this connection it will be necessary to secure the whole hearted cooperation of owners of property and business people so that they will aid in this work by taking care of their own property. This will be one of the things brought up at this meeting and it is hoped that everyone doing business here will attend.

Among the features of entertainment discussed a. this meeting were the following: An old time variety show at the Bird Cage Theater, a free street entertainment on a raised platform between Allen and Toughnut on Fifth Street, a number of exhibits of old time mining equipment, pictures, early day household and business articles, saloon relics, ore specimens and the like, an old time dance to be given in one of the early day saloon buildings, and a street parade and pageant. This street parade will probably be so organized as to depict the founding and growth of Tombstone. First will come Ed Schieffelin followed by other prospectors, Indians, miners, stage coaches, cowboys, covered wagons and other things, on back to the modern automobile.

This is but a bare outline of what will probably take place and it will be the duty of the technical director to build on this program with the aid of local people so as to produce a rapid-fire program of entertainment for visitors from the first day of the show to the last.

It is the belief of the members of the council that this celebration will not only give Tombstone a great amount of advertising but will attract to this place possible investors who may be induced to remain in Tombstone and to make their homes here.

COURTESY OF THE TOMBSTONE EPITAPH NEWSPAPER
JULY 25, 1929

CHAPTER EIGHTEEN

On July 29, 1929, the first Helldorado was sanctioned as an official celebration for Tombstone.

"HELLDORADO" TO BE STAGED OCT. 24 TO 27; PLANS TOLD BY KREBS AT MASS MEETING

Tombstone Making Ready To Welcome Famous Characters Of Early '80's Returning For Four Days

Tombstone's Helldorado fiftieth anniversary celebration will be held from October 24 to 27, inclusive, it was announced by Mayor R. B. Krebs at a mass meeting in the Crystal theater Monday night. The gathering which was well attended by local people, crystalized sentiment whole-heartedly in favor of carrying out the plans to bring back the real, old Tombstone of Ed. Schieffelin's day.

Plans for the unique celebration, already well under way, were given added impetus by the new details brought out at the meeting. Among the many features already outlined for the four days and nights are parades each morning, the real old dance halls and gambling houses opened again, the famous Bird Cage Theater with its old time shows, free special attractions to be given on a platform at Fifth and Allen streets, the main business section of town redecorated to portray the days of 1876, historical exhibits, mining exhibits, and citizens of Tombstone—men, women and children—dressed in costumes of fifty years ago.

The city council is supporting the celebration in every way possible. Mayor Krebs announced. The city will furnish electricity and make changes in the streets necessary to carry out the old-time motif. W. H. Kelly, editor and manager of the Tombstone Epitaph, has been chosen by the council to manage the celebration. George Pound, a professional showman for the past 30 years, will have charge of certain phases of the work, such as choosing suitable actors and arranging concessions suitable to the occasion. Mr. Pound has managed old-time and western shows in Arizona for a number of years and will give the city the benefit of his large experience.

The mass meeting on Monday was opened by Mayor Krebs, who told what has been done, and outlined the work necessary to round out the program. Among those called upon by the mayor for suggestions and opinions were J. A. Ivey, president of the Tombstone Lions club; Mrs. J. H. Macia, A. H. Gardner, manager of the Huachuca Water company, and Sheriff George R. Henshaw. A number of worth-while suggestions were made by the speakers, and will be given consideration by those in charge.

The various committees, 24 in number, were made public for the first time at the meeting. The Honorary Advisory Committee includes such names as Governor John C. Phillips, John P. Clum, founder of the Epitaph and Tombstone's first mayor; Walter Noble Burns, author; William Breakenridge, who served as deputy under John Behan, Cochise sheriff fifty years ago; George H. Kelly, state historian, and others equally well known.

One of the most important committees to local residents will be the "Helldoradoa" charged with enforcing all whisker growing agreements.

COURTESY OF THE TOMBSTONE EPITAPH
AUGUST 1, 1929

Mayor Krebs declared the third weekend in October to be the date of the celebration and officially dubbed it "Helldorado", a term coined by William MacLeod Raines. "Helldorado" was also part of the title of the autobiography of Billy Breakenridge, one of John Behan's first deputies, which was published the previous year. William Kelly's editorial that day was a plea to the townspeople to pull together as a community and to revive the historical significance of Tombstone, which had been taken from granted in recent years.

THE HELLDORADO MEETING

The wholeharted response given Mayor R. B. Krebs at the Helldorado mass meeting held here last Monday night was perhaps the most encouraging thing that has happened so far in conection with this proposed show to commemorate the Fiftieth Anniversary of the founding of the City of Tombstone.

Although the crowd in attendance was not large it was representative of the entire town and the enthusiasm expressed over the plans for the show as announced by Mayor Krebs was unmistakable.

The show as now planned will be a success only if it meets with the approval and gains the support of all citizens of Tombstone. Never before, so far as we have been able to learn, has any town turned its entire business district into a show. Never before has the background for a performance been the streets, the buildings and the equipment of a town itself. The appeal to see a thing of this kind will be a great one and, as Mayor Krebs said at this meeting on Monday, the outside people who visit us will not be disappointed if every business man, every property owner, and every resident does his or her part toward creating the proper atmosphere and background.

It is encouraging also to learn that in spite of the fact that very little has been published concerning this show and that the real publicity campaign has not yet started news from outside visitors and other sources is to the effect that everyone is acquainted with our plans and perhaps several hundred already sent word that they would be here for the show.

"Tombstnoe's Helldorado", will be a great boost for Tombstone. It is hoped that it will be the turning point in the fortunes of this city and that from among the visitors here in October we will gain the first nucleus of a rapidly growing colony of residents who will live here because of our unexcelled climate, scenery and outdoor attractions.

COURTESY OF THE TOMBSTONE EPITAPH NEWSPAPER
AUGUST 1, 1929

Committees were formed to take charge of each aspect of the festival:

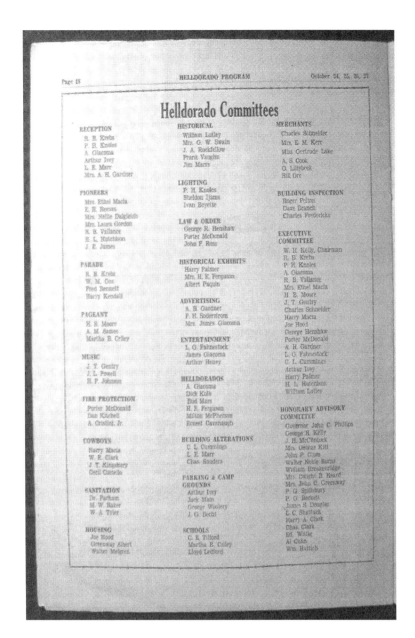

COURTESY OF THE KEVIN & BEVERLY MULKINS COLLECTION

In his August 15, 1929 issue, Kelly carried two noteworthy pieces. The first outlined the incredible progress being made to date. The second was a pair of poignant letters sent to Kelly by John Clum and William Hattich, former owners and editors of the Tombstone Epitaph newspaper.

Historic Old Buildings Now In Hands Of Committee To Assure Helldorado Success

Desperadoes Will Be Kept Within Law By Col. Billy Breakenridge, Who Will Be Sheriff Of Tombstone

That hundreds of former residents of Tombstone, including some who have not been here for close to fifty years, will attend Tombstone's Helldorado is the news being reported to members of the Helldorado committee from every hand.

Recent Tombstone visitors to California and other points report that everyone is enthusiastic over the celebration plans and that the old-timers are especially interested and have all promised to be on hand in October.

Colonel Billy Breakenridge, deputy sheriff here in 1881 and author of the book 'Helldorado', who was a visitor in Tombstone this week from his home in Tucson to look over the Helldorado plans, agreed while here that he would accept the position as "Sheriff of Tombstone" during the celebration and would assist in every way to make the celebration a success. He stated that he is in communication with a large number of former citizens and others who are interested in Tombstone and that he was sure of bringing a large number of prominent people here to see the show.

Actual work on the celebration will be started on September first, according to an announcement made by Mayor R. B. Krebs this week and a meeting of the executive committee has been called for Monday night, September 2. At this meeting the definite program will be laid out and chairman of the different committees will be given an outline of the work each committee will be required to do. Between now and the time of this meeting the members of the executive committee are asked to list the different suggestions they will have to make so that these suggestions can be tabulated and decided upon.

The city council also reported this week that they had definitely secured the use of a number of vacant buildings owned by Mrs. Mary Costello including the famous Crystal Palace Bar." This gives the Helldorado committee the use of all the buildings in the business section that have figured prominently in the history of the city.

The regular advertising campaign over the state will not start in full force until about six weeks before

REPORTS PROGRESS

Mayor R. B. Krebs

siderable work is being done toward sending out the news of the show by letter and in giving Tombstone prominent mention in the press of the state. In every quarter, especially among the newspapers, there is a feeling that Tombstone is deserving of this help and in almost every instance a hearty promise of cooperation has been given.

"In order to make this show a success", Mayor Krebs pointed out this week, "it will be necessary for us to use every old-time relic obtainable. We especially urge local citizens who possess any of these relics, such as saloon pictures, mining equipment, decorations, and the like to inform the committee so that they can be appropriately placed during the Helldorado show."

COURTESY OF THE TOMBSTONE EPITAPH NEWSPAPER
AUGUST 15, 1929

HELLDORADO

What others say about Tombstone's Anniversary Show

John P. Clum, founder of the Epitaph 50 years ago, elected first mayor of Tombstone and honored in other ways by the community of which he was a leading member, has written a most interesting letter, accepting the invitation to serve as a member of the Helldorado advisory committee. Owing to lack of space it is impossible to print the letter in full at this time. In part, it reads as follows:

"Los Angeles, Calif.
"Mr. W. H. Kelly,
Tombstone, Ariz.

"I have served on all sorts and grades and shades and denominations of Tombstone committees, but your suggestion that I serve as a member of the honorary Advisory committee of Tombstone's Helldorado Semi-centennial celebration has a strange weird and formidable aspect.

"My idea of a member of an honorary advisory committee is some venerable person who looks wise and says nothing - although he may do a bit of honoray thinking. Therefore it seems to me that if I am to become a member of your said honorary advisory committe and have anything to say I must say it now, or forever hold my peace.

"As a starter I want to tell you that I am for Tombstone. And I am for Tombstone's Helldorado--provided the celebration can be successfully carried out. Of course, youse fellers have very carefully studied all the 'dips' spurs and agles' of this 'prospect' and have decided that the enterprise can be made a success, otherwise you would not persist in the undertaking. Therefore what ever I may say must be regarded merely as a bit of honorary advisory thinking confidentially conveyed to my typewriter.

"I am not an expert in the show business but I have had some experience. In 1876 I took a bunch of Apaches to 'the states' and we presented a wild and wooly show. The show was a success as a show, but a financial failure. In January, 1890, I was manager of the San Bernardino county (Cal) citrus fair in New York City. The purpose was to introduce California citrus fruits in the New York market. That show was a success. For about ten years while field lecture for the Southern Pacific company I attended many fairs and expositions conducted for publicity purposes. I was 10 months at the Panama-Pacific International Exposition at San Francisco.

"As a rule, the purpose of these fairs and expositions is publicity. In order to make an enterprise of this sort a success you must get the crowd. The next big thing is to accomodate the crowd. If you can get the crowd and make them comfortable and keep them entertained, the crowd will keep on coming in increased numbers and your show will be a big success.

"Of course, I am looking at your proposed celebration from the veiwpoint of one who was there when Tombstone was in the making - was developing after the fashion of a booming mining camp. The 'show' we had to offer was no different from what might be seen in Leadville, or Deadwood, or Pioche, or Virginia City--or any other typical frontier mining camp.

"I thank you for your courtesy and confidence, and for the invitation to attend the show. If my health remains good as it now is I shall plan to help raise Helldorado in Tombstone about Oct. 15th., next.

"Cordially yours
JOHN P. CLUM."

William Hattich, also a former editor of the Epitaph sends the following reply to a simular invitation:

"Los Angeles,
"W. H. Kelly,
Tombstone,

"Your letter just received and note the active work of your committee for the forthcoming Tombstone jubilee.

"The celebration will touch a responsive chord in the heart of every Tombstone pioneer and the spirit of the occasion at once attract to it a host of visitors.

"Tombstone indeed has carved its story in matchless history of the borderland. She has contributed more of colorful romance, tradition and exciting thrills than most other of the historic mining camps in all the west. The magic of its sepulchral name, its intrepid charcters of story and fiction, the glamour of its pioneer fame, and withal, the investing of the many historic spots still intact in Tombstone, where history was made, with a halo of its cherished lore should make of the Helldorado Celebration a momentous occasion, a grand reunion and a magnet of attraction to all.

"With assurances of my hearty best wishes, I am pleased to accept the honor conferred on me by your committee. I am

Sincerely yours,
WILLIAM HATTICH."

COURTESY OF THE TOMBSTONE EPITAPH NEWSPAPER
AUGUST 15, 1929

The most crucial article to appear throughout the summer came on August 29, 1929. In 1903 the railroad had finally come to Tombstone to capitalize on the second silver bonanza between 1902 and 1912. The Southern Pacific Railroad now controlled the tracks in and out of Tombstone. In a move similar to creating a modern-day website, the Southern Pacific Railroad printed 60,000 menus touting Helldorado, which it was estimated would be red by more than 300,000 people.

HELLDORADO STORY TO BE FEATURED ON S. P. MENUS

Tombstone pictures and a write up of the Helldorado celebration will be carried on the menus of the Southern Pacific dining cars during the month of October, according to word received by the committee from the San Francisco offices of the company.

The Southern Pacific is displaying considerable interest in the Helldorado show, and its publicity department has already started giving the event wide-spread notice. A special fare is planned from El Paso and coast points during October 24 to 27, the time of the celebration.

COURTESY OF THE TOMBSTONE EPITAPH NEWSPAPER
AUGUST 29, 1929

As September arrived, the Executive Committee for Helldorado moved into high gear. Mores aspects of the celebration were finalized and announced. At the same time, Kelly began his campaign to retain the Cochise County Seat in Tombstone by keeping the citizens apprised of every detail of the County Supervisor's movements toward relocating it. On September 5, 1929, the Epitaph had these two items prominently displayed on the front page:

DETAILED PROGRAM ADOPTED BY HELLDORADO COMMITTEE; BIRD CAGE TO BE REPAIRED

Elaborate Arches Will Span Allen St. As Main Entrances To Show Area; Crystal To Have New Floor

Actual work on Tombstone's Helldorado show was launched last Tuesday evening when the Helldorado Executive committee held its first meeting at the Community House.

Fourteen members of the committee were present at this meeting and the detailed program for the four day show was worked out. The Executive committee is composed of the chairmen of various Helldorado committees. Each member was given a chance to discuss the work on his particular committee at this meeting and to plan a program of activity for the seven weeks remaining in which to put on the show.

On another page of this issue of the Epitaph this tentative program is being printed in full and suggestions for changes will be discussed at the next meeting of the Executive committee to be held next Monday night. It was also decided to call the Executive committee into meeting every Monday evening at 7:30 from now until the time of the show. It was also decided to invite the citizens of Tombstone to attend these meetings so that they each will secure an understanding of what the Helldorado show will attempt to accomplish.

Members of the committee attending this meeting expressed their enthusiasm as to the possibilities of the show and the fact that local people are anxious to put this show over in a proper manner and to make a name for Tombstone as entertainer and a host.

The actual work of re-building and decoration will not be done until within a week or two of the show in the meantime, a crew of men will be put to work cleaning out and repairing the various empty buildings that will be used, including the Bird Cage Theater and the Crystal Palace. At the Bird Cage the flooring, boxes and front will be repaired and at the Crystal Palace a level floor will be put in to replace the present slanting floor. The Helldorado area was designated as on Allen Street between Fourth and Fifth and between Toughnut and Fremont Street. This area will be blocked off and two elaborate arches will be constructed at the two ends of Allen Street as the main entrances. The arches will extend from the top of the buildings clear across the street and will be properly decorated and lighted.

A number of suggestions for housing were received at this meeting and acting on these suggestions the Housing committee decided to turn the housing concessions over to one man to supply from 200 to 500 cots in vacant buildings and under tents. This, together with private homes and hotels, was considered sufficient to care for the people who will care to remain overnight. It was the opinion of the committee that the largest crowd from Bisbee, Douglas, Tucson, Nogales and the country districts in between would drive back and forth from their homes and would not care to remain in Tombstone over night.

COUNTY SEAT TO BE SUBJECT OF SPECIAL MEETING

Petitions For Removal To Be Submitted, Believed

A special meeting of the board of supervisors has been called by chairman John Hild for 10:00 A. M. Saturday, Sept. 7, in watch it is expected that the question of the county seat removal will be brought up by the filing of petitions from the Douglas district.

The board must fix a date for considering of routine business a recess was declared, and after the special meeting called for Saturday. The board must fix a date for consideration of a special election, providing a sufficient percentage of qualified voters have signed the petition. The legal proceedures will include the necessary publication in three papers of the county for two weeks and the posting of notices in each voting precinct, according to W. E. Clark, clerk of the board.

COURTESY OF THE TOMBSTONE EPITAPH NEWSPAPER
SEPTEMBER 5, 1929

Kelly's next item of significance dispels any of the manufactured, modern-day "legend" of one of Tombstone's most venerable buildings, the Birdcage Theatre.

WORK ON FAMOUS BIRD CAGE WILL START TOMORROW

Dust And Dirt Of 40 Years Will Be Cleaned Out Of Building

VACANT MANY YEARS

Committee Of Old Timers Will Make Survey Of Business Section

Dirt, dust and the accumulated trash of nearly forty years will be cleaned out of the old Bird Cage Opera House, famous in Tombstone history, when a crew of men will be put to work tomorrow preparing the old building for the Helldorado show here next October, according to an announcement made today.

The Bird Cage was first opened for business in 1881 and was at that time operated as a combination saloon, dance hall and variety theater. For ten years it was the center of gay life in Tombstone and was closed in the early nineties when Joe Bignon, the owner at that time moved to the new boom camp of Pearce. Since that time it has been without a tenant and has been used solely as a store room by its present owner, C. L. Cummings. According to Mr. Cummings the building has not been swept out in all that time.

During the Helldorado show, which is being sponsored by the Tombstone city council, this old theater building will be reopened and three performances daily will give the modern theater fans a taste of old time acting. Young actors and actresses, however, will be used and once again for the first time in two score years the Tombstone nightingale will bring cowboys and miners to their feet in the Bird Cage.

Besides the Bird Cage all the other historic buildings in the camp will be reopened and more than $10,000 will be spent in bringing the old camp back to life for a few short days.

TO MAKE SURVEY

In order to rebuild old business sites and landmarks to make Tombstone as nearly as possible the same as it was in the days of its prime in 1880 when it was the largest city in Arizona, for the Helldorado days a general survey is to be conducted within the near future by Colonel Billy Breakenridge of Tucson, John A. Rockefelow of Cochise Stronghold, William Lutley, C. L. Cummings, Jim Marrs and Mrs. G. W. Swain all of whom were residents of Tombstone in 1880.

It is the plan of the members of the Tombstone city council, to rebuild and sign the business in such a manner as to prevent a true to life picture of the famous mining camp as it appeared 50 years ago.

The plan for the celebration is to allow the people of Arizona and nearby states a taste of olden days as they were lived in the west and because of the fact that most of the main business houses and dwellings remain the same as they were in 1880 it will give the show an aspect that will be in no way an imitation.

COURTESY OF THE TOMBSTONE EPITAPH NEWSPAPER
SEPTEMBER 12, 1929

The article also states that $10,000.00 had been raised to restore the historic buildings back to their 1880's stature. "Colonel Billy Breakenridge of Tucson, John A. Rockfellow of Cochise Stronghold, William Lutley, C.L. Cummings, Jims Marrs, and Mrs. G. W. Swain all of whom were residents of Tombstone in 1880," would assist the committee to insure authenticity in the restoration. September 13th was designated as the day to clean up the "dirt, dust and accumulated trash of nearly forty years," in the Bird Cage Theatre, which it says had been used as a "store room" by its owner C.L. Cummings since Joe Bignon closed it in the early 1880's.

HELP IS NEEDED

In another column of the Epitaph is a notice given us by Mr. Harry Palmer, chairman of the Helldorado exhibits committee, asking that owners of early day relics who would care to put these relics on exhibit during the Helldorado show get in touch with him at once. These relics will be placed in a convenient and safe location for exhibition during the show and every precaution will be taken to insure their safe return to the owners.

There is also a notice in this issue of the Epitaph to the effect that local people who do not care to make or assemble their own costumes for this show will be able to rent costumes at a resonable price through Mr. Charles Schneider who has consented to act as costuming agent for the Helldorado committee without profit to himself. One of the greatest helps local people will be able to give the Helldorado committee will be to help in furnishing local color during this show by wearing the garb of fifty years ago. The ladies especially can help in this way and with all Tombstone people in costume the spirit of the show will not be hard to put over to the thousands of visitors who will come here. The local men can dress as cowboys, freighters, miners, gamblers, troopers or prospectors while the ladies can vary their dress from the plain cotton dress worn on the covered wagon to the more elaborate costume of the ball room and theater.

Those desiring costumes should place their orders at once so that they will be received in plenty of time.

---o---

COURTESY OF THE TOMBSTONE EPITAPH NEWSPAPER
SEPTEMBER 12, 1929

On September 19th the paper announced that Mrs. Nettie Vail, Ed Schieffelin's niece, and Mrs. Gulrado, his sister, would be in attendance for the event. The Executive Committee, as well as the whole community of Tombstone was keenly aware of the shortage of hotel and restaurant accommodations in the town in 1929. Ingenious solutions were implanted thanks to the Arizona National Guard and, again, Southern Pacific Railroad.

STATE GUARD TO LOAN EQUIPMENT FOR HELLDORADO

Use Of 700 Cots, Blankets Are Part Of Plans For Visitors

More than 700 cots and blankets will be supplied the Tombstone Helldorado committee by the Arizona National Guard to assist in housing the hundreds of people who will attend the Helldorado Show to be held in Tombstone October 24, 25, 26 and 27, according to an announcement made by Joe Hood, chairman of the housing committee.

These cots, according to Hood, will be used to increase the capacity of local hotels and will also be placed in private homes. Others will be used in buildings that are now vacant but which will be converted by the Helldorado committee into temporary hotels.

The housing committee is also in communication with the Southern Pacific company in the hope of securing twenty-five or thirty Pullman cars together with two or three diners to be used in housing part of the crowd. A favorable report has been received on this but definite arrangements have not yet been made. These housing preparations, Hood said, are being made to care for the hundreds of people from outside of Arizona who have already indicated their intention of seeing Helldorado. The greatest number of visitors, he said, would come from Tucson, Nogales, Bisbee and Douglas and most of these will probably return home each night even though they see more than one day of the show.

Sketches showing the necessary changes in a few of the business buildings in order to place them in the same condition as they were in the 80's have been completed and a crew of carpenters and painters will start on this work before the end of the month. Most of the buildings, however, will require no touching up except for the removal of modern signs since more than twenty of them including the famous old Bird Cage and the Crystal Palace Bar, are the old original structures.

Old time residents are assisting the Helldorado committee in making the changes so that they will be historically accurate and every effort will be made to faithfully reproduce the Tombstone made famous by Colonel Billy Breakenridge, Sheriff Johnny Behan, Wyatt Earp, John Ringo, Buckskin Frank Leslie and the half hundred more who lived here in the early days.

COURTESY OF THE TOMBSTONE EPITAPH NEWSPAPER
SEPTEMBER 19, 1929

The following week, Kelly again blended two key historical elements in to his weekly update.

WHISKEY WILL HAVE NO PART IN HELLDORADO

Officers To Cooperate With Executive Committee In Keeping Show Clean

FOX TO MAKE MOVIES

Celebration Scenes Will Be Released In Movietone News And Westerns

That bootleggers, bad whiskey and drunks will be kept out of Tombstone so far as possible during the Helldorado Show was definitely decided on at the last meeting of the Helldorado Executive committee held last Monday night at the Community House.

Speaking of this situation which will undoubtedly come up during the show Mayor R. B. Krebs stated that the crowd would be too large and the program too big to permit the confusion and disorder that would undoubtedly arise should no effort be made to keep the drinking question well in hand. This sentiment was also expressed by Sheriff George R. Henshaw and he stated that his office would show no mercy to bootleggers or drunks caught in Tombstone during the celebration. It was officially decided to notify the federal prohibition forces of this action on the part of the Helldorado committe and to ask their cooperation in the matter.

Good Progress Made

That the Helldorado Show is progressing in great shape and that all will be ready in plenty of time for the show was revealed in the various reports of the committee chairmen who are now actively engaged in getting their work into shape. The Pageant Committee reported that they had fully arranged their program and that they would be ready to go in advance of the Helldorado dates. Other committees reports similar progress and assured the executive committe that in every way possible last minute confusion will be eliminated.

Work of preparing false fronts for local buildings will be started this morning by Jack Gamble, official decorator and they will be ready in plenty of time to put up within a few days of the show. In the meantime several signs will be made to identify the various buildings and historical scenes.

To Film Show

A letter received by the Helldorado committee yesterday from the New York offices of the Fox Movietone people states that they have made arrangements for the filming of Helldorado for news reel purposes and that their represenative would be here during the Helldorado dates. They are also planning on taking several scenes here to be used later on in western pictures.

The free street acts and the Bird Cage Show have not all been booked as yet but several good acts are being considered and within the next two weeks will be signed up on contract. Effort is also being made to secure an old time medicine show for one of the vacant lots.

Hundreds of letters pouring into Tombstone from every side stating that visitors from every part of the continent will be here assures the Helldorado show of a tremendous crowd for the four days and since most of them are from former residents and pioneers the prediction is that Helldorado will be able to boast of the greatest gathering of Arizona pioneers ever held in this state.

COURTESY OF THE TOMBSTONE EPITAPH NEWSPAPER
SEPTEMBER 26, 1929

Mayor Krebs and Cochise County Sheriff George R. Henshaw made it <u>very</u> clear that Helldorado and Tombstone would strictly enforce the Volstead Act prohibiting alcohol (the Crystal palace Saloon had been restored, but the only beverages sold would be soda pop). More significantly, Krebs announced that Fox Movietone Newsreels and Pathe Films would be in attendance with film and sound crews to document this historic event. The next week, October 10, 1929, Kelly again worked his layout magic as the headline read:

COMMITTEES IN READINESS FOR THE BIG SHOW

PROGRAM FOR HELLDORADO ALMOST COMPLETE WITH ALL DEPARTMENTS WELL IN HAND

Professional Entertainers, Bird Cage Troupe, Medicine Show, Pageant, Parade, Banquet, Dances, Games, Scenes And Costumes Arranged For

With a crew of carpenters and decorators busy building over the business district of Tombstone to give it the appearance of this historic old town in the eighties, a total of twenty four professional entertainers signed for the Bird Cage Theater, a medicine show and free street shows and the big parades and pageants outlined and scheduled Tombstone's Helldorado Show, October 24 to 27 is practically ready for the thousand of people who are expected to visit here during that time.

COURTESY OF THE TOMBSTONE EPITAPH NEWSPAPER
OCTOBER 10, 1929

In almost equally large font was the following:

ELECTION ON REMOVAL SET FOR NOV. 19

Compromise Date Fixed By Supervisors; Tax Money To Provide Funds

Tuesday, November 19, has been set by the board of supervisors as the date for a special election to determine whether the Cochise County court house shall remain in Tombstone, or be moved to a new location selected by the electors.

The special meeting of the Supervisors last Saturday was for the purpose of veiwing the election and taking action upon it. The date of November 19 was deemed a compromise between the score of Douglas citizens present, with Supervisor John Hild of Douglas asking for an election at the end of 30 days, and Supervisor Harlie Cox, Bisbee who request that the election be held not earlier than the first Tuesday in December. Supervisor Walker, Willcox, split the difference but an agreement was not reached until some presure was brought to bear on members of the Douglas delegation, who were a single unit in demanding an early election.

Tombstone representatives objected to the requests of Douglas on the grounds that an election held in 30 days would interfere with Helldorado celebration and also the state fair.

An objection was entered by attorneys from Tombstone that the election could not be carried out at this time as there was no money available in the county treasury. After some discussion it was brought out by Supervisor Harlie Cox of Bisbee that there was $4500 in the treasurer's office that had been recently collected for back taxes, which had not been anticipated in the 1929-30 budget.

Under a recent ruling by the supreme court and the attorney general of the state, Cox pointed out, money that was not appropriated in the budget, but was in the county treasury, could be used for any lawful purpose or for any debts incurred. Therefore it was not deemed necessary to ask for an emergency to hold the proposed election, as the board had no choice, it being mandatory by law to call the election when a hearing was held on a petition and it was found to be aquate and proper. This action was taken by the board on the advice of the county attorney James T. Gentry, but to satisfy all concerned the board requested that the county attorney take up the matter with the attorney general of the state. The county attorney was also asked to obtain an opinion from the attorney general as to who is qualified to vote at the election.

In discussing the forthcoming election, Supervisor Harlie Cox stated that the Warren District Welfare association has held several meetings on the subject of the removal of the county seat, and are rapidly becoming organized to protect Bisbee's interests in the matter.

Douglas was represented by 25 and 30 leading citizens among whom were Mayor A. C. Karger, Rex Rice, Sam Applewhite, Arthur Curlee, Attorney W. P. Gilmore, J. P. Sexton, D. C. O'Neal, George Dawe, Russell Meadows, Douklas Cooper, and several others. Bisbee was represented by S. G. Pummer and Frank Thomas.

COURTESY OF THE TOMBSTONE EPITAPH NEWSPAPER
OCTOBER 10, 1929

Kelly also took this opportunity to place the following editorial dead center on page one:

MAKE HELLDORADO A SUCCESS

That Tombstone's Helldorado is assured of a great success is attested to by the hundreds of letters now being received by local people and the Helldorado Committee from every part of the country. The letters speak enthusiastically of the show and in most cases the writers plan to be in attendance.

Helldorado is a tremendous undertaking for a community the size of Tombstone but with local people entering into the spirit of the occasion with greater enthusiasm each day, the work of the various committees is going ahead in proper shape and they report everything well in hand. The important question of having local people appear in costume during the show is being taken care of in fine shape by the people themselves and from present indications there will be no lack of cowboys, cowgirls, gamblers, miners, troopers, society people, dance hall girls and every other early day character known in Tombstone during the eighties.

With this year's Helldorado a success it is to be hoped that local people will see fit to continue it as an annual or bi-annual event and make of it a typical Tombstone institution drawing more and more people to this place every year.

COURTESY OF THE TOMBSTONE EPITAPH NEWSPAPER
OCTOBER 10, 1929

Locals practiced the famous fight on Fremont Street between the Earps, "Doc" Holliday and the "Cowboys", Ike and Billy Clanton along with Frank and Tom McLaury. All of the preparations were being completed ahead of schedule. Those residents who were not performing, stayed busy making their own period costumes, and many of the men grew beards for the occasion. A grand parade with john P. Clum, former mayor of Tombstone and founder of the Epitaph newspaper, along with Billy Breakenridge would lead the procession as honorary Mayors. The Yuma Indian Marching band was committed to play in the Helldorado parade. The Pickwick Papers carried a story which includes this description,

"Nowadays the town has slumped, due to the flooding of the mines that were its life and soul. But around October 24, Tombstone is going to re-awaken a few days of its old life---minus the alcohol and murder, or course."

The next issue of the Epitaph came out on Tuesday, October 15, 1929, and Kelly returned his editorial to page eight.

FIFTY EVENTFUL YEARS

Fifty eventful years have gone by since John P. Clum sounded "The First Trumpet" in the first issue of the Epitaph in 1880. During those years the fates have been particularly kind to Cochise county and following the great discovery at Tombstone other rich and prosperous communities grew up to make of Cochise the second richest county in Arizona.

The Epitaph and Tombstone—the largest paper and the largest city in all Arizona at one time—have both seen the greatest period of any within the knowledge of the human race. Briefly this period has covered stupendous changes in the relations of individuals, and nations which themselves in some instances have completely reversed their forms of government. Crowns have fallen, thrones crashed; America has grown into the most powerful nation of the earth; in many ways its dictum is more weighty today than that of all of the other civilized peoples combined. Marvelous inventions and discoveries have changed the course of human life and the trend of thought; ideals have changed; the world is better than it ever was, and the American people as a whole, are more prosperous, enlightened and have higher ideals, than any people at any time in the history of civilization.

Fifty years ago Tombstone was entering upon a career which was to make of it the most talked of town in all the west. Events have transpired during those fifty years which could happen in no other period and in no other place. A great mining district was developed, thousands of people were brought here from the four corners of the earth and the present industrial development of the State of Arizona must date from the discovery of the great Tombstone mines and the consequent attraction to this state of men, money and publicity.

From the end of its first burst of glory, close to fifty years ago, however, Tombstone has had an unceasing struggle to maintain its existence. Water in the mines, slumps in the silver market, high costs of transportation before the coming of the railroad, numerous county seat removal fights and a hundred minor difficulties have conspired to test the mettle of Tombstone citizens and but for their constant vigilance and unceasing energy together with the loyal support of nearby friends Tombstone would long since have joined the ranks of twenty other early day towns that flamed and died away.

No sooner will this great Helldorado Show end than the handful of citizens who have stuck loyally with this historic town be called on to fight again the ever present menace of county seat removal.

We believe that Tombstone will meet this new menace and win over it as it has met and won her other battles. That we are not alone in the fight and that our old-time friends will again come forward with every possible assistance will add new vigor to our efforts. It is hard for us who know and love Tombstone to believe that a handful of selfish landowners can induce the people of this county to destroy the town that gave us our start.

COURTESY OF THE TOMBSTONE EPITAPH NEWSPAPER
OCTOBER 15, 1929

Another wonderful piece of history was also on that page:

COURTESY OF THE TOMBSTONE EPITAPH NEWSPAPER
OCTOBER 15, 1929

Tombstone had a baseball team from 1882 until 1929. As the article points out, they were one of the best in the southwest. The importance of this piece is that this is one of the many C. S. Fly [photographs that are missing, but Kelly had access to it in 1929 (apologies for the poor quality, but it is difficult to secure a quality photograph from microfilm). Throughout this issue Kelly mixed in reprints of articles from Tombstone's past. He announced that all was ready for the extravaganza in nine days.

HELLDORADO WILL BE RE-CREATION OF OLDEN TIMES

Parade Of Old Timers Will Be Special Feature Of 4 Day Celebration

BIRD CAGE IS OPENED

Breakenridge, Clum Among First Citizens Taking Part In Program

Swinging saloon doors, the whir of the roulette wheel, festive miners and cowboys watching the vaudeville show in the Bird Cage Opera House, rough men gathered on the street corner, a few quick, hard words, the crash of a revolver—then silence. And silence in the old buildings for two generations, broken at last by the surging throng of visitors to Tombstone's Fiftieth Anniversary Helldorado celebration.

Saloon doors will again creak and swing, the roulette wheel will spin again, accompanied by the song of "Round an) round the little wheel goes; where she tops they's nobody knows", heavily rouged beauties will reappear on the Bird Cage stage.

Tombstone citizens have been planning organizing, arranging a suitable program for all who care to take part in the semi-centennial fiesta of the at one time, leading city of Arizona Territory. Pioneers are especially welcome, but everyone is invited, the Helldorado executive committee has announced.

And many old timers have stated that they will be on hand. John P. Clum, editor and founder of the Tombstone Epitaph, Tombstone postmaster and mayor, will act as Mayor of Tombstone again and once more take the editorial chair. Col. William Breakenridge, former deputy sheriff under John Behan in the early eighties, will be Sheriff of Tombstone, and many others who played parts in the unfolding drama of southwestern history will return. Countless others will never return, for they lie in their last long sleep, after heroically carving niches for themselves in pioneer annals.

Self Advertising

The rebirth of the town, a town made possible by Ed Schieffelin's untiring perseverance, offers elements so unique that it has advertised itself, purely on the ground of news. For the Helldorado celebration is to be an actual rebirth of old times, old scenes and the daily life of 50 years ago. Nothing is being left undone, committee members report, to make the show true to life, and newspapers over the west have found the unusual in many episodes of early Tombstone.

The present town as well as the former thriving city is known best to countless thousands as seen thru the eyes of authors who have gathered local material for stories, articles, biographies and novels. Alfred Henry Lewis, William McLeod Raine, Walter Noble Burns, William Breakenridge, Lorenzo D. Walters, Anton Mazzanovich, William R. Burnett, Will Levington Comfort—these are a few of the men who have written or are writing of the happiness and sorrow, the comedy and tragedy once enacted in old Tombstone.

The first tentative program, as adopted by the Helldorado executive committee in September, has been rearranged, added to, and improved so that it now represents hardly more than an outline of the complete celebration in detail. Among the innumerable features of interest will be thrilling free street acts, a parade of pioneers, performances in the Bird Cage, a museum of priceless relics and mementos, many early incidents reenacted true to life, old fashioned miners' rock drilling contests, hose cart races, a pageant, saloons reopened, dance halls and gambling games running full blast and many other things.

The parade in itself will be unique, with the famous old Modoc stage, a faithful adherance to the costumes of the eighties, with women riding on side saddles, burros carrying ore, prospectors with their equipment and innumerable other details to portray the times. J. A. Rockfellow, who followed a pack animal on a 500 mile trip through the territory 50 years ago, is one of the many pioneers who will take part.

Many To Take Part

Among the many old timers in addition to those already mentioned who are helping to make the celebration the success it will be are Dave Adams and William Poorr, both pioneer cattlemen; Jeff Milton, early day peace officer and famous for bringing home his man; William Lailey, freighter and cattleman for many years; C. L. Cummings, Tombstone business man since 1880 and present owner of the Bird Cage theater and other buildings of historic interest; relatives of Ed Schieffelin and William Monmonier, early day citizen and at one time justice of the peace. Lack of space forbids the mention of a hundred others, some of whom will be assembled for the last time for swiftly advancing years are dealing harshly with those who fought the Apaches, hunted outlaws, and finally brought a measure of peace to the hard won land of the southwest.

Complete arrangements to feed and shelter hundreds of visitors who wish to remain during the entire four days have been made. Hundreds more will bring camp equipment and bedding, while others will bring only bedding, for cots and beds will be available as long as space remains unsold.

Glimpses of the Past

Nothing beyond a bare idea of Tombstone's re-creation can be presented in print; but to those who knew and lived the old days, the statement that Helldorado will be the old Tombstone will suffice. To others, glimpses of the past would perhaps explain the show better. Rolling back the curtain we see:

Wyatt Earp holding off an infuriated mob of 300 men who wanted to lynch "Johnny-Behind-the-Deuce" a lone man against an infuriated gang of rough characters who packed Allen street from one side to the other. A single barrel and two glittering eyes finally dispersed the men, many of whom were armed.

"Nigger Jim" who boasted that he was one of the first "white" men to come to Tombstone and stake out a claim. A notorious bad man jumped the property and Jim calmly met him at his own game, giving the town a good laugh. The coroner's jury met the approval of popular sentiment with the verdict "—and served him right for getting in front of the gun."

Four men, three of them Earp brothers and their companion, the greatly to be remembered Doc Holliday, stalked along Fremont street, finally coming to a stop before four cowboys near the rear entrance to the O. K. Corral. Guns blazed forth, killing three and wounding two others, and bringing to a climax the long smoldering Earp-Clanton feud.

Holdups Galore

The old Modoc stage left Tombstone for Benson, the railroad point. Outlaws suddenly opened fire near the crest of a hill, killing the guard on top, but frightening the horses so that they ran away and saved the Wells Fargo strong box. Other and more successful holdups were staged on the Benson road, on the road to Bisbee, and almost everywhere that bandits heard of valuables being transported in time to plan a daring coup. Dead stage hands, dead desperadoes, and sometimes dead passengers were numbered in those who finished the journey.

Such dramas made southwestern history—these and countless other happenings brought Tombstone's name before the world. For the re-creation of the olden times Mayor R. B. Krebs, the city council, and practically every citizen of the slumbering old mining camp have been busy for weeks and months.

Helldorado awaits you.

"—WITH PICK AND CANTEEN PLACED BESIDE HIM—"

(Prospector, June 4, 1897) A dispatch from Oakland says: "The will of Ed Schieffelin was opened yesterday. The will made provision for burial in the park of a prospector, on the granite hills three miles westerly from Tombstone, and a monument erected over his grave such as prospectors erect to mark the location of a mining claim. He asks none of his friends to wear crepe. He leaves $75,000 to his widow and brother."

(Epitaph, Jan. 21, 1882) Mr. Ed Schieffelin is examining the gold fields of Alaska.

COURTESY OF THE TOMBSTONE EPITAPH NEWSPAPER
OCTOBER 15, 1929

CHAPTER NINETEEN

Finally the day arrived and the headlines read:

WELCOME TO HELLDORADO

COURTESY OF THE TOMBSTONE EPITAPH NEWSPAPER
OCTOBER 24, 1929

Throngs of people had come from all over the world to celebrate this momentous occasion. The entire business district had been given a facelift. New paint and repairs were imperceptible to the visitors, but the effect was almost perfect. The City of Tombstone was shining brightly in the southern Arizona desert. 343 of the over 400 pioneers invited were in attendance. This in itself is one of the greatest compliments a community could receive. It also validates that Tombstone was not the bawdy, dangerous, uproariously wild town late in the development of the western frontier. It was a modern, sophisticated Victorian city with every luxury and modern convenience available in the 1880's. These pioneers firmly believed, at the time, that Tombstone was destined to become the next San Francisco. It was a place of great wealth and great dreams.

The citizens of Tombstone had prepared a schedule of events to whet the appetites of their guests. Three old-time shows each day were given in the venerable Bird Cage Theatre, except for the first day. There were some electrical issues that prevented the initial show, but the others all came off without a hitch. The archways at each end of Allen Street welcomed locals and tourists alike. Souvenir programs detailed the daily events. The schedule was the same for each day, but no one seemed to care. On Friday, October 25, 1929,

Pioneer Day, a ceremony was held three miles west of town at the burial site of the town's founder, Ed Schieffelin. Ed Schieffelin discovered silver in the hills that surround Tombstone, and in spite of the inherent danger from the elements and the Apaches, he and his brother Albert, and Richard Gird began mining these hills in 1878. The settlement that sprang up alongside their mining operation became a village called Tombstone in 1879. That morning proper acknowledgement and homage was paid to this simple man they all called "Ed".

COURTESY OF THE TOMBSTONE EPITAPH NEWSPAPER
OCTOBER 31, 1929

HELLDORADO PROGRAM

THURSDAY, OCTOBER 24, 1929

10:30 A. M. CEREMONY AT SCHIEFFELIN MONUMENT in memory of Ed Schieffelin and other Tombstone pioneers. At close of ceremony rockets from nearby hills officially opens Helldorado

10:45 A. M. THE THREE TANTLINGERS in an exhibition of trick shooting, trick roping and other stunts on the Helldorado street platform.

11:45 A. M. BIG PARADE. (See Page 17). Featuring old time vehicles and other interesting relics. Parade forms at Harry Macia residence immediately following monument ceremony. March to Allen Street, through Helldorado to High School and back. Earp-Clanton fight immediately after parade on Fremont Street at O. K. Corral.

2:00 P. M. STAGE COACH HOLD-UP. Old Modoc stage is held up by Chiricahua outlaws and Wells Fargo box looted. Corner Allen and Fifth Street near platform.

2:30 P. M. BAND CONCERT by famous Yuma Indian Band.

3:00 P. M. FIRST SHOW at Bird Cage Theater opens. (See Page 9).

3:00 P. M. HELLDORADO WRESTLING TOURNAMENT

3:20 P. M. JACK and VIRGINIA SCHALLER. Adagio athletes, platform act.

3:50 P. M. BELL & BELL TROUPE. Four people, head and hand balancing; platform act.

4:15 P. M. VIERA BROTHERS. High and aerial rings and trapeze act; platform act.

4:40 P. M. JOE, JACK, and GEORGE. Comedy acrobats doing table rock and fall on platform.

5:00 P. M. BELL THAZER TROUPE. Five people in big specialty act on 100-foot tower inside Helldorado area.

5:30 to 7:30 P. M. All concessions and buildings open.

6:30 P. M. BAND CONCERT by famous Yuma Indian Band

7:00 P. M. FIRST EVENING PERFORMANCE at Bird Cage Theater opens. (See Page 9).

7:30 P. M. THE THREE TANTLINGERS. Four platform acts including trick roping, trick shooting, combination roping and boomerang throwing.

8:00 P. M. HELLDORADO BOXING TOURNAMENT.

8:00 P. M. JACK AND VIRGINIA SCHALLER. Adagio athletes, platform act.

8:30 P. M. BELL & BELL TROUPE. Four people head and hand balancing, platform act.

9:00 P. M. SECOND EVENING PERFORMANCE at Bird Cage Theater. (See Page 9).

9:15 P. M. VIERA BROTHERS. High and aerial rings and trapeze act; platform act.

9:45 P. M. JOE, JACK and GEORGE. Comedy acrobats doing table rock and fall on platform.

10:15 P. M. BELL THAZER TROUPE. Five people in big specialty act on 100-foot tower inside Helldorado area.

FRIDAY, OCTOBER 25, 1929

10:30 A. M. EARP-CLANTON FIGHT. A re-enactment of this famous street battle on Fremont Street at O. K. Corral gates.

11:00 A. M. BIG PARADE. (See Page 17). Featuring old time vehicles and other interesting relics. Parade forms at Harry Macia residence at 9:30 a. m. Visitors are asked to leave Helldorado area and watch parade from sidewalks west of Helldorado on paved street.

11:30 A. M. PIONEERS' BANQUET. Pioneers asked to gather at Schieffelin Hall for noon meal.

1:30 P. M. PARADE OF PIONEERS ONLY. Parade forms at Schieffelin Hall and marches through Helldorado area. No vehicles or horses.

2:00 P. M. STAGE COACH HOLD-UP. Old Modoc stage is held up by Chiricahua outlaws and Wells Fargo box looted. Corner Allen and Fifth Street near platform.

2:30 P. M. BAND CONCERT by famous Yuma Indian Band.

3:00 P. M. FIRST SHOW at Bird Cage Theater opens. (See Page 9).

3:00 P. M. HELLDORADO WRESTLING TOURNAMENT

3:20 P. M. THE THREE TANTLINGERS. Four platform acts including trick roping, trick shooting, combination roping and boomerang throwing.

3:50 P. M. JACK and VIRGINIA SCHALLER. Adagio athletes, platform act.

4:15 P. M. BELL & BELL TROUPE. Four people, head and hand balancing, platform act.

4:40 P. M. VIERA BROTHERS. High and aerial rings and trapeze act; platform act.

5:00 P. M. JOE, JACK, and GEORGE. Comedy acrobats doing table rock and fall on platform.

5:20 P. M. BELL THAZER TROUPE. Five people in big specialty act on 100-foot tower inside Helldorado area.

5:30 to 7:30 P. M. All concessions and buildings open.

6:30 P. M. BAND CONCERT by famous Yuma Indian Band.

7:00 P. M. FIRST EVENING PERFORMANCE at Bird Cage Theater opens. (See Page 9).

7:30 P. M. THE THREE TANTLINGERS. Four platform acts, including trick roping, trick shooting, combination roping and boomerang throwing.

8:00 P. M. HELLDORADO BOXING TOURNAMENT

8:00 P. M. JACK and VIRGINIA SCHALLER. Adagio athletes, platform act.

8:30 P. M. BELL & BELL TROUPE. Four people, head and hand balancing; platform act.

9:00 P. M. SECOND EVENING PERFORMANCE at Bird Cage Theater. (See Page 9).

9:15 P. M. VIERA BROTHERS. High and aerial rings and trapeze act; platform act.

9:45 P. M. JOE, JACK, and GEORGE. Comedy acrobats doing table rock and fall on platform.

10:15 P. M. BELL THAZER TROUPE. Five people in big specialty act on 100-foot tower inside Helldorado area.

COURTESY OF THE KEVIN & BEVERLY MULKINS COLLECTION

SATURDAY, OCTOBER 26, 1929

10:30 A.M. EARP-CLANTON FIGHT. A re-enactment of this famous street battle on Fremont Street at O. K. Corral gates.

11:00 A.M. BIG PARADE. (See Page 17). Featuring old time vehicles and other interesting relics. Parade forms at Harry Macia residence at 9:30 A. M. Visitors are asked to leave Helldorado area and watch parade from sidewalks west of Helldorado on paved street.

2:30 P.M. STAGE COACH HOLD-UP. Old Modoc stage is held up by Chiricahua outlaws and Wells Fargo box looted. Corner Allen and Fifth Street near platform.

2:30 P.M. BAND CONCERT by famous Yuma Indian Band.

3:00 P.M. FIRST SHOW at Bird Cage Theater opens. (See Page 9).

3:00 P.M. HELLDORADO WRESTLING TOURNAMENT

3:20 P.M. THE THREE TANTLINGERS. Four platform acts including trick roping, trick shooting, combination roping and boomerang throwing.

3:50 P.M. JACK and VIRGINIA SCHALLER. Adagio athletes, platform act.

4:15 P.M. BELL & BELL TROUPE. Four people, head and hand balancing, platform act.

4:40 P.M. VIERA BROTHERS. High and aerial rings and trapeze act; platform act.

5:00 P.M. JOE, JACK, and GEORGE. Comedy acrobats doing table rock and fall on platform.

5:20 P.M. BELL THAZER TROUPE. Five people in big specialty act on 100-foot tower inside Helldorado area.

5:30 to 7:30 P.M. All concessions and buildings open.

6:30 P.M. BAND CONCERT by famous Yuma Indian Band.

7:00 P.M. FIRST EVENING PERFORMANCE at Bird Cage Theater opens. (See Page 9).

7:30 P.M. THE THREE TANTLINGERS. Four platform acts, including trick roping, trick shooting, combination roping and boomerang throwing.

8:00 P.M. HELLDORADO BOXING TOURNAMENT.

8:00 P.M. JACK and VIRGINIA SCHALLER. Adagio athletes, platform act.

8:30 P.M. BELL & BELL TROUPE. Four people, head and hand balancing; platform act.

9:00 P.M. SECOND EVENING PERFORMANCE at Bird Cage Theater. (See Page 9).

9:15 P.M. VIERA BROTHERS. High and aerial rings and trapeze act; platform act.

9:45 P.M. JOE, JACK, and GEORGE. Comedy acrobats doing table rock and fall on platform.

10:15 P.M. BELL THAZER TROUPE. Five people in big specialty act on 100-foot tower inside Helldorado area.

SUNDAY, OCTOBER 27, 1929

10:30 A.M. EARP-CLANTON FIGHT. A re-enactment of this famous street battle on Fremont Street at O. K. Corral gates.

11:00 A.M. BIG PARADE. (See Page 17). Featuring old time vehicles and other interesting relics. Parade forms at Harry Macia residence at 9:30 A. M. Visitors are asked to leave Helldorado area and watch parade from sidewalks west of Helldorado on paved street.

2:00 P.M. STAGE COACH HOLD-UP. Old Modoc stage is held up by Chiricahua outlaws and Wells Fargo box looted. Corner Allen and Fifth Street near platform.

2:30 P.M. BAND CONCERT by famous Yuma Indian Band.

3:00 P.M. FIRST SHOW at Bird Cage Theater opens. (See Page 9).

3:00 P.M. HELLDORADO WRESTLING TOURNAMENT

3:20 P.M. THE THREE TANTLINGERS. Four platform acts including trick roping, trick shooting, combination roping and boomerang throwing.

3:50 P.M. JACK and VIRGINIA SCHALLER. Adagio athletes, platform act.

4:15 P.M. BELL & BELL TROUPE. Four people, head and hand balancing, platform act.

4:40 P.M. VIERA BROTHERS. High and aerial rings and trapeze act; platform act.

5:00 P.M. JOE, JACK, and GEORGE. Comedy acrobats doing table rock and fall on platform.

5:20 P.M. BELL THAZER TROUPE. Five people in big specialty act on 100-foot tower inside Helldorado area.

5:30 to 7:30 P.M. All concessions and buildings open.

6:30 P.M. BAND CONCERT by famous Yuma Indian Band.

7:00 P.M. FIRST EVENING PERFORMANCE at Bird Cage Theater opens. (See Page 9).

7:30 P.M. THE THREE TANTLINGERS. Four platform acts, including trick roping, trick shooting, combination roping and boomerang throwing.

8:00 P.M. HELLDORADO BOXING TOURNAMENT.

8:00 P.M. JACK and VIRGINIA SCHALLER. Adagio athletes, platform act.

8:30 P.M. BELL & BELL TROUPE. Four people, head and hand balancing; platform act.

9:00 P.M. SECOND EVENING PERFORMANCE at Bird Cage Theater. (See Page 9).

9:15 P.M. VIERA BROTHERS. High and aerial rings and trapeze act; platform act.

9:45 P.M. JOE, JACK, and GEORGE. Comedy acrobats doing table rock and fall on platform.

10:15 P.M. BELL THAZER TROUPE. Five people in big specialty act on 100-foot tower inside Helldorado area.

COURTESY OF THE KEVIN & BEVERLY MULKINS COLLECTION

BOOK HELLDORADO
BOOK TOMBSTONE

True Histories of Tombstone For Sale

Only at

COURTESY OF THE KEVIN & BEVERLY MULKINS COLLECTION

You'll Find Your Tombstone

WITH ONLY thirty dollars in his pocket but equipped with a fairly good prospecting outfit Edward Schieffelin struck out from San Bernardino California, in the spring of 1877 for Arizona. At Hackberry in the Hualpai country, he found a scouting party just setting out for the southern part of the Territory to scout down there for Apaches. Schieffelin went along with the soldiers, so that he might prospect in the Apache infested region under their protection. The expedition reached the Huachuca mountains, April 1, 1877, and while the soldiers were making preparations for a scouting trip, Schieffelin scoured the neighboring hills, returning to camp each night. When the troops started out, he went with them. But he could not accomplish much in this way, so he soon detached himself from the scouts and went alone among the hills bordering the San Pedro. He continued to use Fort Huachuca as a base, however.

"Have you found anything," the soldiers would ask him, as he came back now and then.

"Not yet," he would reply, "but I will find something some day."

"Yes. You'll find your tombstone," they would retort.

"The word remained in my mind," Schieffelin writes, "and when I got into the country where Tombstone is now located, I gave the name to the first location I made. Upon the organization of the district it was called Tombstone from that location."

The discovery of good float led Schieffelin to the decision to gain the aid of his brother who was then in northern Arizona and the result of this was the formation of a partnership with his brother, Al and Dick Gird, a well known mining man.

A complete outfit was brought in from Tucson and soon after their arrival Ed made the strike that was to make him famous. One morning while Gird remained at the house to do some assaying, Ed and Al went to a spot where Ed, a day or two before, had picked up a very pretty piece of ore that carried a good deal of gold, and began to trace it up. They were out of fresh meat, and Al suggested that Ed go kill a deer. But this day Ed's soul was hectic with expectation and suspense. The fires of genius were aglow in the heart of the prospector; he felt rather than knew that success was in his grasp.

Find Rich Mine

"There's no use for me to go, because I can't kill anything today. You'd better go and kill the deer, and I'll try and trace this ore up."

In the afternoon Al returned with the deer. Ed had found where the ore came from and was building a monument.

HELLDORADO AUTHOR

They brought specimens to the cabin. Gird took one piece that looked very good to him, and breaking it open found it full of horn silver. The next day Gird and Ed went to the spot where Ed had secured his specimens and located the Lucky Cuss Mine. This was the strike that made Tombstone and made Schieffelin famous.

Soon the news got loose that Gird and the Schieffelins had struck it rich, and people were now pouring into the Tombstone region. Wild rumors were afloat. There were strikes here and strikes there. The big boom was on. Gird and the Schieffelins were opening up their claims, and some of them were turning out exceedingly well.

In April, 1878, the Schieffelins and Gird sold their rights in the Contention to White and Parsons for $10,000, and the mine made these men rich. The Tough Nut, the Lucky Cuss, and several other claims were thrown into a company and the share the Schieffelins held in this was sold by them for $600,000 in 1880. The product of their mines ran into the millions and around these mines was built the greatest frontier town of the early eighties—rivaling San Francisco in splendor and extravagance.

COL. WILLIAM BREAKENRIDGE

Dies While Prospecting

Ed Schieffelin was a prospector to the end. May 14, 1896, while he was out on a prospecting trip he died alone in the doorway of his cabin about twenty miles east of Canyonville, Oregon. It was his desire that his remains—

COURTESY OF THE KEVIN & BEVERLY MULKINS COLLECTION

COURTESY OF THE KEVIN & BEVERLY MULKINS COLLECTION

COURTESY OF THE KEVIN & BEVERLY MULKINS COLLECTION

The gala event came off without a hitch. A grand time was had by all who attended. On October 31, 1929 William Kelly published an issue of his paper with a myriad of accounts and descriptions of the four-day celebration.

STREET BATTLES THRILLING PART OF CELEBRATION

Fight Between Earps And Clantons Re-enacted At O. K. Corral

MURDERER LYNCHED

Famous Old Modoc Stage In Realistic Holdups Once Again

The more thrilling parts of the four-day Helldorado program, such as stage coach hold-ups, street gun battles and hangings, furnished the most vivid features of Tombstone's semi-centennial birthday celebration, according to comments made by visitors each day of the show. Such grim episodes seemed to appeal particularly to those who had feared something of the town's eventful history and attended Helldorado for the purpose of learning more.

Re-enacted on the blood stained ground at the Fremont entrance to the O. K. Corral, the Earp-Clanton feud each day drew an enormous crowd which packed the street for a solid block. Every detail of the notorious fight which took place in October 48 years ago was followed, the most authentic facts having been collected from eye witnesses as well as contemporary accounts which appeared in the Tombstone Epitaph and Daily Nugget of 1881.

From the moment Sheriff Johnny Behan attempted to get the Clantons and McLowerys to leave town until the final corpse was carried away the crowd watched breathlessly. Innumerable still pictures of the fight and many moving picture films were used in recording the re-enactment.

A lane was kept clear along the south side of Fremont to the Fourth street corner. At a signal the action started with Sheriff Behan (W. A. Tyler) approaching the cowboys, and searching them for arms. Two of the men kept their guns, the others claiming they were unarmed. Behan then left in search of the Earps to attempt to dissuade them from picking a quarrel. He met Virgil, Wyatt and Morgan in company with Doc Holliday, approaching the other group.

Pushing him to one side and paying no the slightest attention to his protests, the Earps and Holliday walked on. Suddenly guns flamed out on both sides, because so quick that bystanders could not follow the details. Within a few seconds, just as it happened almost 50 years ago, Frank and Tom McLowery were slain, 19 year old Billy Clanton was mortally wounded and Ike Clanton had escaped through the Corral. Two of the Earps were slightly injured, while the other one and Doc Holliday, exponent of the sawed off shotgun, were untouched.

Almost equally thrilling was the holdup of the Modoc stage, an early afternoon feature each day. Spectators watched intently as masked bandits halted its journey and forced passengers to alight and line up beside the road. They were searched in an expert manner, the express strong box and the mail sacks were taken, and then the robbers rode away, only to be routed at last by a pursuing posse. The terror of many of the passengers was extremely realistic, especially that of a musician with the medicine show, who consented to act as passenger on top of the coach each day.

An episode staged at four o'clock each afternoon on Allen street was also very realistically played. In this scene a grizzled prospector, crazed from thirst and loneliness, staggered into town, mumbling to himself. In one hand he clutched a bag of gold and with the other dragged his rifle and an empty canteen. In an altercation with desperadoes who had arrived, one pulled a gun. The prospector drew a bowie knife, but was shot down in his tracks. A posse, hurriedly sworn in, left on the trail of the murderer, and soon returned with him, securely manacled. A convenient pole and a rope provided the requisites for lynch law and the man was hanged in a throughly realistic and workmanlike manner.

HELLDORADO SIDELIGHTS

William S. (Broncho Bill) Bartlett, who was among the many Helldorado visitors, came to Arizona Territory in 1874, filling the duties of guide and scout with Colonel, later General Miles. Mr. Bartlett also served as messenger during the early days, and for some time was chief scout, with almost 40 Indian scouts under his command. He is a resident of Tucson at present, and Mrs. Alli eDickerman, his daughter, is postmaster of the Old Pueblo. Mrs. Dickerman also registered at headquarters during Helldorado.

H. C. Stillman, early day Cochise county peace officer and contemporary with Col. William Breakenridge, met many old friends at pioneers' headquarters on Allen street while attending Helldorado. Mr. Stillman, Col. Breakenridge, for the first time in many years while seeing Tombstone's fiftieth birthday, in the course of subsequent conversation they discovered that they each held an honorary life membership card in the Elks lodge. They both served as deputies under Johnnie Behan, first sheriff of the county. Mr. Stillman was one of the first subscribers to the Epitaph.

Mrs. J. J. Monteverde, accompanied by her husband John J. Monteverde, vice chairman of the advisory board, bank of Italy, Sacramento, Calif., was one of the old time pioneers who returned to Tombstone to take part in the Helldorado. Mrs. Monteverde, nee Sophie Jones, was a child when she and her family were citizens of the scoring silver camp of the southwest.

Mrs. Dave Joanis, Glendale, Calif., met Mrs. Monteverde on the train from Los Angeles to Tombstone's fiftieth anniversary celebration, and they discovered that they had known each other here when both were little Miss Joanis, formerly Miss Mae Mugan, left the camp 43 years ago, not to return until Helldorado was in full swing last week. Mrs. Joanis and Mrs. Monteverde recalled many of the better known episodes during Tombstone's early life, for they were residents of the thriving city at that time.

Mrs. Mugan, mother of Mrs. Joanis, operated the Aztec House in Tombstone almost a full half century ago. Miss Laura Mugan, sister of Mrs. Joanis is living. Mrs. Joanis and Mrs. Monteverde both stated that it was the call of the Helldorado revival which caused them to return to old Tombstone. They noticed many changes in the town, particularly in some of the buildings, and also noted many more evidences of similarity with the camp when it was very young.

S. J. (Gus) Tribolet, Phoenix, in Tombstone for the Helldorado show, met many old friends while here and recalled many incidents of early days in and around Tombstone, when talking over the lurid old times with others. He built the Crystal Palace saloon during the eighties, at that time the largest saloon in Arizona Territory. Mr. Tribolet came to Arizona in 1879, and is now a prominent Phoenix business man.

COURTESY OF THE TOMBSTONE EPITAPH NEWSPAPER
OCTOBER 31, 1929

That issue listed all 343 pioneers that returned to Tombstone for the festival. The first segment appears below, with the remainder on the subsequent page. It is an impressive list to say the least.

Names Of 343 Pioneers In State More Than 30 Years Ago Written In Register During Helldorado

Of the hundreds of pioneers who registered at Helldorado headquarters during the four-day celebration of Tombstone's fiftieth birthday, a total of 343 came to Arizona more than 30 years ago. Owing to the great number who registered it is impossible to publish the entire list this time, but the names given below are those who came to Arizona Territory in 1898 or before. The name, present address, and date of arrival in Arizona are given:

Edward L. Vain, Tucson, 1879; E. T. Jones (Blinky,) Tucson, 1879; J. M. Hennessy, Flagstaff, 1879; R. T. Fenter, Tucson 1887; Mrs. George Kitt, Tucson, 1878; Mrs. Mattie Riggs Johnson, Elgin, 1876; Mary E. Cumins O'Brien, Santa Monica, 1881; E. J. Schieffelin, Pasadena, 1884; Thomas Cummings, Santa Monica, 1881; Ralph Fettereg, 1880; Mrs. J. M. Monteverde, Sacramento, 1881; Mrs. Mae V. Jonas, Glendale, 1880; Mrs. Laura Sparks, Riverside, 1898; Mary A. Blackburn, Tombstone, 1882; Ray Swain, San Francisco, 1880; Mrs. George W. Swain, Tombstone, 1880; George M. Swain, Los Angeles, 1880; Melvin W. Jones, 1875; Mrs. Abbie A. Gilbert, Phoenix, 1881; D. A. Adams, Dragoon, 1879; Mrs. H. W. Stewart, Phoenix, 1882; Mrs. A. W. Smith, Tucson, 1887; William Pearce, Tucson, 1882; Mrs. Lydia A. Thiel, Tombstone, 1891; Mrs. Elizabeth McPherson, 1884.

J. A. Rockfellow, 1890; Charles L. Blackburn, 1889; Mrs. Francis Larriu Conyers, Tombstone, 1889; Mrs. L. Lurriu Chadwick, 1870; A. D. Page, Nogales, 1896; E. M. Webb, 1881; Richard Farrell, Jr., Naco, 1890; John Meadows, Jr., Douglas, 1898; Virginia Martin, Hereford, 1882; Har-

(Turn To Page Four)

COURTESY OF THE TOMBSTONE EPITAPH NEWSPAPER
OCTOBER 31, 1929

Horn Snodgrass, 1884; Anie Hughes Dahle, 1882; May Jones Hancock, 1882; D. K. Hancock, 1882; Berry Gneable, 1887; Mrs. John Slaughter, 1879; Glen McLaughlin, 1894; P. C. Kinsey, 1881; Mrs. Patty Lombardi, Tombstone, 1873; Mrs. J. N. Johnson, Lowell, 1878; Mrs. M. C. Hazelwood, Bisbee, 1882; Edith M. Stow, 1873; Mrs. William Lutley, 1883; Mr. and Mrs. M. J. Cunningham, 1891-1893; Ives Bogan, Los Angeles, 1881; John Campbell, 1894; Mrs. John Campbell, 1889; Georgia Phelps Boucher, 1878; Mrs. H. C. Stillman, 1889; John Hennessy, 1873; E. A. Hughes, Charleston, 1882; E. A. Willig, 1882; Camels Wallace, 1882; I. W. Wallace, 1883; Mrs. Elmer D. Harder, 1894; J. E. Corey, Charleston, 1881; Edith Robertson, Mac'a, 1854; Nellie M. Dalgleish, 1882; Mary Tibrien, 1883; Mrs. Ena Pennepacker, 1881; Lizzie Cenach Schofield, 1882; Esther Rafferty Brown, 1883; C. W. Hicks, 1882; Mrs. Mary Hicks, 1885; David A. Mackone, 1894; Mrs. Annie Matthews, 1899; Jane Critchley Perier, 1880; Ray swain, 1890; B. C. Tarbell, 1882; D. S. Chamberlain, Ives Moizer, Ia., 1879; Edith Hughes Pacheco, 1882; Sara D. Curtis, 1881; George Sherrer, Dragoon, 1878; Mrs. George Sherrer, Dragoon, 1880.

Mrs. Guy Emmons, Benson, 1891; Mrs. Donus M. Fitch, 1882; J. W. Van Horn, 1880; E. K. Thomas, Tombstone, 1879; Haley Thomas, Tombstone, 1882; E. J. Griffin, Bisbee, 1885; John N. Bright, Tucson, 1882; John C. Phillips, 1892; Mrs. John C. Phillips, 1895; Mr. and Mrs. Peter Carpentelo, Phoenix, 1881; Mrs. Dave Adams 1872; Dora E. McDougall, Patagonia, 1882; Manuel Mogis, Jr., Tucson, 1881; B. G. Long, Nogales 1885; E. G. Adams Burkett, Texas, 1885; Frank B. Reis, Hallbrook, 1885; L. Caldwell, Hallbrook, 1896; G. J. Hibb, Patagonia, 1888; Jerry Sheehy, Patagonia, 1878; Elizabeth Hamilton, Tucson, 1888; Mrs. John Towner, Naco, 1884; John Towner, Naco, 1894; Henry Karl Steele, Aje. 1885; K. J. Tribolet, Phoenix, 1878.

E. J. Handa, Phoenix, 1887; Mrs. Althea Ford, Tombstone, 1881; Mrs. Sylvia Welch, Tombstone, 1880; Mrs. M. C. Bravin, Los Angeles, 1880; C. Feuney, Chicago, 1894; Mrs. E. Farrell Harshaw, 1883; Mrs. Hazza Harshaw, 1888; Neil Erickson, 1883; Mrs. Neil Erickson, 1883; Mrs. Mary F. Earnes, St. David, 1881; John S. Merril, St. David, 1878; Mrs. H. Kempf Benson, 1880; Mrs. Eva Hendrerson, Patagonia, 1882; Mrs. H. C. Stillman, Douglas, 1880; Mrs. W. E. Hankba, Bisbro, 1896; Mrs. John Slaughter, Douglas, 1879; Edith M. Stone, Douglas, 1879; Earl Reed, Douglas, 1891; Park Allison, Tucson, 1875; C. L. Cummings, Tombstone, 1880; Mr. and Mrs. Ed. M. Riggs, 1889; Mrs. Pattie Welch, Tucson, 1884; Fred M. Welch, 1889; Kirk L. Hart, Tucson, 1884; Mr. J. C. Gibson, Nogales, 1881; J. C. Gibson, Nogales, 1881; Mrs. R. D. Thurston, Los Angeles, 1881; Florence Riggs McGregor, Tucson, 1877; Hilda Kramer, Tucson, 1889; Anna Schafer Lahm, Bowie, 1879; B. R. McGregor, Tucson, 1886; Mrs. John Nowell, Naco, 1894; Mrs. Frank Penderson, Bisbee, 1896; Mrs. George M. Dowdle, Naco, 1890; Mrs. Mary Shibell Brown, Tucson, 1890; Lillie M. Schibell, Tucson, 1880; Annie Rockfellow, 1896; Mrs. Annie Watkins B'shee, 1887; Mrs. Nellie Henderson, Bisbee, 1883; Mrs. Ben Daniels, Tucson, 1882; Mrs. J. K. Brown, Tucson, 1882; James K. (Bay) Brown, Tucson, 1882; Marguerite Brown Stroud, Tucson, 1889; Ada E Jones, Nogales, 1884; Laura Blacklidge, Tucson, 1881; H. J. Blacklidge, Tucson, 1882; Edna

BANKHEAD BARBER SHOP
SCALP TREATMENT
Massaging, Shampooing Hair Cutting and Trimming
A. H. ENDSLEY   Tombstone
Manager   Arizona

Dr. C. A. McNeir Chi.
Now located at Willard Hotel Tucson. The famous McNail cancer treatments and other

Hughes Morse, Phoenix, 1888; Mrs. Charles Pickhill, Phoenix, 1896; William R. Bartlett, Tucson, 1874.

C. T. Howard, Warren, 1881; Mrs. W. S. Bartlett, Tucson, 1888; Mrs. Allie Dickerman, Tucson, 1896; C. J. Frank, Tombat on, 1882; Charles De Sauf, Tucson, 1875; H. C. Stillman, Douglas, 1880; Mr. and Mrs. Thomas A Stafford, Dos Cabezas, 1890; Mrs. J. N. Christensen, St. David, 1880; J. N. Christensen, St. David, 1880; Mrs. J. Davis, Tucson, 1885; J. W. Smith, Tombstone, 1882; C. B. Myers, 1878; W. W. Adams, Dragoon, 1896; Jack Harris, Bisbee, 1897; J. J. Muirhead, Bisbee, 1881; A. E. Abbott, Pearce, 1887; Mrs. L. J. Lemons, Pearce, 1882; Mrs. W. J. Lindenfeld, 1888; Mrs. Hulda Lippert, Tombstone, 1881; Mrs. E. R. Parsons, Phoenix, 1882; Mrs. Winnie Jowles, Bisbee, 1896; Charles Wilson, Bisbee, 1893; Moss Drachman, Tucson, 1872; Mrs. Moss Drachman, Tucson, 1871; Mrs. P. E. English, Pearce, 1879.

Mr. and Mrs. G. A. Eisenhart, Pearce, 1884; Mrs. Fred Clifford, Pearce, 1889; R. J. Euglika, Pearce, 1883; Alfred Hickwood, Phoenix, 1882; Fred Clifford, Dos Cabezas, 1882; Geo. K. Smith, Phoenix, 1889; Stanley Kitt, Tucson, 1881; Andrew P. Martin, Tucson, 1884; Lee Joranevich, Bisbee, 1891; Mrs. Jilda Bishop, Bi. David, 1894; L. W. Douglas, 1894; Mrs. J. S. Douglas, Douglas, 1889; J. P. Richardson, Dragoon, 1886; Mrs. K. W. Gale, Contention, 1881; Winifred Gravotta, Tucson, 1892; Warren A Grovetta, Tucson, 1883; Raymon Abel, Tombstone, 1896; Tomas Moumier, 1884; Mrs. Caterine Long Crowan, 1886; J. F. Eisenhart, Pearce, 1895; L. K. Caveza, Benson, 1877; M. P. Lofgreen, Benson, 1888; B. A. Navarro, Tucson, 1873; Mr. and Mrs. F. C. Roberts, Tucson, 1878-1881.

Frank W. Fish, Tucson, 1879; C. H Krosser, Tucson, 1887; Mrs. M. Webster, Douglas, 1894; Mrs. Marion Gannon, Bisbee, 1898; J. F. Murphy, Pearce, 1885; H. C. Dickson, Phoenix.

ARCADE HOTEL
Mrs. J. H. Maple
ENTIRELY RENOVATED
Hot and Cold Water
SHOWER AND TUB BATHS
Phone 70

FIRST CLASS GUNSMITHING PROMPT SERVICE
OLDHAM SPORTING GOODS COMPANY
Tucson   Arizona

DR. A. E. CRUTHIRDS
Eye, Ear, Nose and Throat
GLASSES FITTED
Office over Bank of Bisbee, Bisbee
Office Hours 9:30 to 12 and 2:30 to 5:30. Office Phone 911. Residence Phone 249.

and have dinner at the OWL where only quality food is served.

aft, 1881; H. H. Brophy, 1881; Minnie Sauer Shilling, 1877; Marguerite R. Shillins, Benson, 1896; I. R. McCloskey, 1894; Mrs. E. B. Henderson, Tucson, 1889; George P. Kiel, Tucson, 1881; Harry A. Morgan, Phoenix, 1889; Carl W. Buss, Tucson, 1896; Mr. and Mrs. George W. Sherrer, Webb, 1884; J. C. Bishop, Tombstone, 1886; E. A. Wadkins, St. David, 1888; J. Baker, Douglas, 1882; A. J. Harmon, Safford, 1896; Dr. I. B. Hamilton, Cananea, 1891; Ralph Morris, Patagonia, 1880; Elizabeth Parker Brown, Nogales, 1892; Frank J. Duffy, Nogales, 1889; Mrs. Nemie Wilson, Solomonville, 1894; Mrs. Ira Williamson, Solomonville, 1896; Herbert C. Blair, Bisbee, 1890; Josephine C. Roemer, Benson, 1879; Sam Coleman, Sonora, 1881; Sophia Castaneda, Tombstone, 1881; Mrs. T. J. Spaulding Foster, Bisbee, 1897; A Roemer, Benson, 1893; J. Fred Black, Solomonville, 1895; C. Castaneda, Nogales, 1880; J. B. Grant, 1896; James Marris, 1879; A. M. Franklin, 1875; W. T. Roach, Elgin, 1892; P. J. Baffer, 1889; Mary T. Greene, 1887; Mrs. L. D. Redfield, Benson, 1884; Leonard R. Redfield, Benson, 1878; Mr. and Mrs. W. A. McDonald, Bisbee, 1890; Ruth G. Kelly, 1895; Mrs. W. A. Grahe, Tucson, 1880; W. A. Grahe, Tucson, 1887; R. P. Carpenter, Phoenix, 1896; Mr. and Mrs. F. A. Vidarro, Bisbee, 1888.

Mr. and Mrs. R. Caretto, 1879; Mrs. Goldtree Woolf, 1886, Tucson; Alice Campbell Joint, Warren, 1881; C. A. Bainti, Los Angeles, 1890; Ruth Pennington Fowler, Tucson, 1891; J. G. Peterson, Mesa, 1883; H. Rasmussen

Hawley & Hawley
Successors to COLE & CO.
937 12th St.   Douglas, Arizona
Box 4,   El Paso, Texas
Assayers, Chemists
SMELTER REPRESENTATIVES
CAREFUL ATTENTION GIVEN SHIPMENTS TO EL PASO AND DOUGLAS SMELTERS

NOTICE!
The name of the Cottage Hotel has been changed to FREMONT HOUSE.
25 Nice Clean Rooms
Apartment and 4 Garages
Reasonable Rates
Opposite High School
Mrs. A. Gristy & Co. Props.

Tucson, 1889; Tom Kurtz, 1884; Mrs. Tom Kurtz, 1894; Isaac Jacobs, Bisbee, 1897; Harold sykes, Tombstone, 1894; Mrs. Mary Muddy, Pearce, 1882; Mrs. Howard Boulter, Bisbee, 1882; Joe Mulrhead, Bisbee, 1881; Ed. L. Howell, Mesa, 1882; J. J. Frazier, Mesa, 1879.

FROM DOUGLAS
Mrs. James Vestori of Douglas visited Charles Schnieder and family during the Helldorado.

TOURIST HOTEL
JOE HOOD, Proprietor
"On the Broadway of America"
Tombstone   Arizona

NOW OPEN!
HERB McDONALD
Opposite Cochise County State Bank
EXPERT TIRE REPAIRING & VULCANIZING
Oiling and Greasing
GAS
OIL
WATER & AIR
Tombstone   Arizona

1925 Standard 6 Coach. A-1 paint and motor. Priced for a quick sale.
1926 Overland Coach. A fine car for a small family. Price $195.
1925 Hudson 7 Passenger Sedan. Priced for a quick sale at $250.
Buy With Confidence Under the Famous Studebaker Pledge
Open Evenings.
Buy With Confidence
All Above Cars Sold Under Our Thirty Day Guarantee

Bisbee Motor Co., Inc.
Upper Main Street—Phone 5
Bisbee, Arizona

STOVES—
STOVEPIPE—
COAL BUCKETS
—o—
We have what you need to keep that house warm this winter.
—o—
OUR LINE OF GROCERIES
AND CHOICE MEATS IS COMPLETE

A. Cristini

Kelly added one last editorial on page eight of that issue:

HELLDORADO BUT A BEGINNING

It is appropriate but next to impossible at this time to express editorially the gratitude of the Helldorado Committee for the countless favors extended Tombstone and Helldorado before and during the celebration last week. It was rare indeed when this committee was refused a favor from any source and it was unquestionably this spirit of cooperation and helpfulness that made Helldorado what it was.

We believe that local people must realize now the value of their town as a tourist attraction and although the attendance was not as great as it would have been under better weather conditions it would be conservative to say that five million American people read of this show and now have a desire, however latent, to see the town in which the show was held.

Helldorado was a success if the accomplishment of an original idea makes for success. The idea behind the show was to crystalize the volumes of publicity written around Tombstone in recent years. We believe that this was done and now comes the biggest job of all .... doing something about it. We all know of the existence of the Mammoth Caves of Kentucky, the tombs of Egypt and the skyscrapers of New York but it takes more than the mere knowledge of the existence of those things to force us to pack up and go visiting. People now know about Tombstone. We have successfully advertised the name and romance of our town and locality. Now we must make a visit here an attractive prospect and we must be prepared to properly entertain the visitors when they do come.

Helldorado has merely opened the way for bigger jobs in the future.

COURTESY OF THE TOMBSTONE EPITAPH NEWSPAPER
OCTOBER 31, 1929

Unfortunately for Tombstone, the inaugural day of Helldorado, Thursday, October 24, 1929 was "Black Thursday" when the stock market crashed. The glorious reviews of the daily activities could not offset the financial disaster that had struck the nation. Kelly and Krebs' hopes for rejuvenating Tombstone's economy through tourism never came to fruition as the nation spiraled into the Great Depression. William Kelly went from "quarterback" to "cheerleader" without missing a beat. He understood that the events over those four days were designed to be a foundation for Tombstone's future, not the finished construction of a 50th Anniversary. In addition the threat of the County Seat removal still loomed less than three weeks ahead.

To the extent that Helldorado had renewed the public's awareness and interest in Tombstone, the event was a tremendous success. It did reestablish the town's place in history from a national perspective and, more importantly, a local standpoint. The impact was powerful enough to make the County Supervisors concerned about the upcoming special election on the County Seat removal. On November 7, 1929, page eight had this note from Kelly to his readers:

DON'T BE MISLED

The members of the board of supervisors of Cochise county, notoriously unfriendly to Tombstone, must now take the front rank position among those who, by one route or another, fair or unfair, would move the court house to Douglas.

We find in the official proceedings of the board of supervisors the following paragraph:

"Chairman John Hild announced that he wished to go on record that in event the County Seat was not removed at the Special Election to be held on November 19, 1929 the Board of Supervisors should take immediate steps to build a new Court House in Tombstone. Member Walker stated that he was of the same opinion. Member Cox being called upon stated that he had contended from the first that in case the County Seat was not moved the County should make adequate provisions to house the offices located outside the Court House."

Mr. Hild's "going on record" and Mr. Walker's hasty second in this matter are little short of an insult to the intelligent taxpayers of this county. Their action means but one thing: An effort to swing votes in favor of Douglas that would otherwise vote for non-removal to save the cost of a new building. It is an insult because they know and the people of Tombstone know and every other taxpayer and voter in Cochise County who is acquainted with the facts know that the construction of a new court house building in Tombstone would be both foolhardy and a criminal waste of the taxpayers' money.

Five minutes investigation on the part of any voter in this county will convince him that there is not only adequate room under the present arrangement for the transaction of county business but that the court house building is in perfect structural condition, comfortable, airy and entirely satisfactory in every regard. He will also find that offices outside the court house building are as close to the other county offices as they would be if they were housed together in a large building and that there is neither inconvenience or any costly loss of time in communication between offices.

It is probably true that these three men would have the power to erect a new building provided no one protested. It is one thing to have this power and an entirely different thing to exercise it. The people of Cochise County have too high a regard for justice to allow any three men throw their good money away in this manner regardless of what the statutes say.

The people of this county cannot be misled so easily. A vote for non-removal means a continuation of the present arrangement, no added tax burden, no fancy real estate schemes and the end of all county division talk.

COURTESY OF THE TOMBSTONE EPITAPH NEWSPAPER
NOVEMBER 7, 1929

Consequently, on November 19, 1929, the voters of Cochise County elected to move the County Seat to Bisbee, where it still resides today.

BSTONE, COCHISE COUNTY, ARIZONA. THURSDAY, NOVEMBER 21, 1929.

LOCAL CITIZENS LOSE FIGHT FOR COUNTY SEAT WITH BISBEE AND DOUGLAS VOTING FOR REMOVAL; BISBEE WINS FOR LOCATION

EARLY RETURNS PUT BISBEE IN LEAD FOR PLACE

Record Vote Is Cast In All Precincts To Win On Removal

TOMBSTONE ENDS AS COUNTY SEAT AFTER 50 YEARS

Three Cornered Fight Ends In Shift To Center Of Population

COURTESY OF THE TOMBSTONE EPITAPH NEWSPAPER
NOVEMBER 21, 1929

According to SPPN, who has the rights to the Pathe newsreel film, no footage still exists. Fox Archivist, Peter Bregman in New York, believes the newsreel footage of the first Helldorado probably never made it to the theaters due to the stock market crash. Today, out of four days with film and sound crews, there are 1.39 minutes of the Fox Movietone Newsreel left. It is curated by the University of South Carolina in Columbia, South Carolina.

The importance of this moment in Tombstone's history cannot be overlooked. Two men, William Kelly and Mayor Ray B. Krebs, took one vision; pulled an entire community together for the sake of their town; organized and raised the necessary financing to transform Tombstone back to its original luster. Regardless of the motives, economic or political, for 96 hours Tombstone was again the jewel of the Old West mining towns, without the whiskey or murder, of course.

HELLDORADO REVIVED

By HARRIET W. HANKIN

The old days! The old life!
Old Helldorado town
Draws back the curtain from her past,
Resumes her silver gown.
Old scenes renew their frontier guise,
Lost faces once more show,
Old words and deeds revive the West
Of fifty years ago.

The old West! The wild West!
The West of rope and gun:
Rough cowboys shooting up the town—
Mere Helldorado fun;
Bold outlaws thumbing noses at
Faint-hearted, futile Law;
And Justice siding with the man
Who's quickest on the draw.

The old doors, the green doors,
Aswing both night and day;
The tense, enthralling poker games,
The tricky roulette play.
Their elbows on the polished bar,
A motley group we scan:
The tenderfoot, the tin-horn cheap,
The deadly two-gun man.

The old guns! The six-guns!
The Earp and Clanton feud;
The flaming guns of Curly Bill,
And all his outlaw brood.
Twelve notches Buckskin Frank displays,
Thanks to his lightning draw;
Now comes John Slaughter, sheriff staunch,
Whose gun enforces law.

The old road, the rough road,
With dust and chuck-holes cursed;
The heat and glare of desert sun,
The rage of desert thirst;
Behind the rocks Apaches lurk —
Red fiends with purpose fell;
Yet risk and hardship help to weave
Old Tombstone's luring spell.

The old charm, the wild charm,
The magic and the thrill,
Cling yet to each enchanted street,
And glamour-haunted hill.
Romance and Luck stretch siren hands,
Adventure calls to youth,
The spirit of the vivid past
Returns in very truth.

But old hopes, and high hopes,
And Love and Friendship true,
Imbued this hetic atmosphere
With earnest purpose, too.
Life throbbed in full; its echo yet
Through years of silence beats —
A soundness cadence that we sense
In Tombstone's ancient streets.

TOMBSTONE, ARIZONA
MOST NOTORIOUS OF THE EARLY MINING
CAMPS IN THE SOUTHWEST

A HEAVY SNOW STORM COMES TO TOMBSTONE, ARIZONA, ONCE IN MANY YEARS. NOTICE DEPTH OF SNOW. THIS STORM CREATED A HOLIDAY SPIRIT IN THE OLD CAMP.

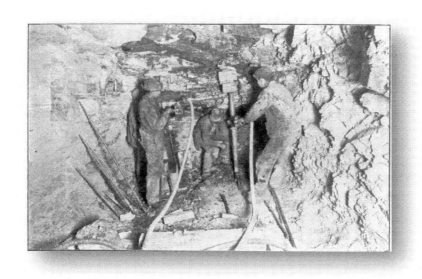

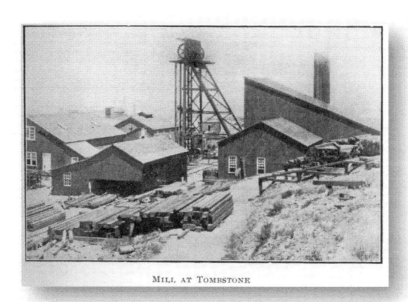

MILL AT TOMBSTONE

Made in the USA
Monee, IL
26 September 2022

b73cd2cd-fd7f-4041-8ef5-6ab6ee37094eR01